Pressure Cooking
for Every Occasion

Pressure Cooker Basics

Introduction to Fagor Pressure Cookers

Thank you for purchasing a Fagor Pressure Cooker. We appreciate the confidence you have placed in our company by selecting one of our many pressure cookers, and we are confident that it will give you many years of excellent service.

Fagor has been making pressure cookers for more than 50 years. All models feature three safety valves plus a locking handle that prevents opening under pressure, so the cooking experience is completely secure. In addition, all our models are beautifully designed with an exterior polish mirror finish, and are constructed of 18/10 stainless steel with an aluminum encapsulated bottom for even heat distribution, work on all types of domestic stovetops – gas, electric, ceramic or induction, are U.L. approved and come with a 10-year consumer warranty.

What are the Benefits of Pressure Cooking?

fast. Saves up to 70% in cooking time!

easy. Just load the ingredients and liquids into the cooker, close the lid, bring to pressure and cook, then release and open the lid. It's that simple!

healthy. Because foods are cooked under pressure, up to 50% more vitamins and minerals are retained. Also, shorter cooking times retain more nutritional values of food.

safe. Fagor Pressure Cookers have three safety valves that permit any possible excess pressure to escape, so the cooking experience is completely secure.

versatile. All types of food can be cooked in a pressure cooker – from vegetables, rice, stews, soups, chicken, fish, meats & even desserts.

energy efficient. Because pressure cooking reduces cooking times, this means a conservation of energy.

great taste. The steam created inside the cooker breaks down the fibers in food in a very short time, leaving food moist and succulent, with an intense intermingling of flavors.

How does my pressure cooker work?

When the lid is properly locked into place onto the cooker, an airtight seal is created. As the liquid inside the cooker becomes hot, it reaches an internal cooking temperature up to 250°F (at High: 15 psi setting). Steam is then created and the pressure begins to rise. If you have a Fagor model that has different pressure settings, the cooking temperature reached inside the pressure cooker will vary depending on the pressure setting you've selected. All Fagor pressure cookers are equipped with a spring valve pressure mechanism.

What are the benefits of a spring valve pressure mechanism?

As pressure builds in the pressure cooker, a spring-loaded valve located in the lid compresses and raises a visual pressure indicator into an upright position. Depending on the type of Fagor Pressure Cooker model you have purchased, pressure levels may be indicated with numerical markings- 1 LOW/ 8psi and 2 HIGH/15psi. While other models with one pressure setting will show an image of a pot which indicates a HIGH setting /15psi.

What are some tips before I begin Pressure Cooking?

To ensure that everything is in working order, it's important to check all the parts of your Fagor Pressure Cooker every time you use it.

Here's what to check:

Make sure the pressure cooker is washed well after the last use. There should be no food or residue on the pot or lid. Make sure the inner part of the lid rim, the outer rim on the pot, and the gasket, are clean. This will reduce the risk of the lid sticking when you open the pressure cooker after cooking.

Remove the gasket to make sure that it is still flexible and is not dried out. Check for any tears or cracks. If the gasket shows any sign of being dry or damaged, do not use the pressure cooker.

Replace the old part immediately with a new gasket, readily obtainable by shopping online at www.fagoramerica.com, or by calling our Customer Service Department at 1-800-207-0806.

Check the safety valves. All current Fagor pressure cooker models have a spring-regulated valve. Press or pull gently on the valve to make sure that it moves without any resistance. Since each model design may vary slightly, check your Fagor user's manual for the exact requirements for keeping the safety valves in working order.

How do I load my pressure cooker?

Because a pressure cooker needs space for steam to be created and room for the pressure to build, never fill your cooker more than 2/3 full. Never pack solid foods into the cooker, as it would defeat the purpose of fast cooking. When preparing meat and poultry for cooking under pressure, brown them, without the lid on, directly in the pressure cooker. By doing so, you will be adding flavor to the dish as well as adding extra color by browning the meat or poultry first. Always brown with the lid off and usually over high or medium-high heat, in order to sear the surface. Marinated foods should be well drained. All meat and poultry should be patted before browning. When browning, be careful that the burner is not too high or you will burn the oil and scorch the pot. Do not deep fry in a pressure cooker, regardless of whether the lid is on. When steaming foods, lightly coat the surface of the steamer basket you are using. Foods, like fish, have a tendency to stick to the surface. When done steaming, remove the food from the steamer basket immediately.

Positioning and Locking the Lid in Place:

Once all the ingredients are in the cooker, you can begin cooking. To open the lid, slide the safety lock to the open position. Turn the lid counterclockwise until the raised indentation on the lid is lined up with the base handle.

Building and Adjusting Pressure:

To build pressure in a pressure cooker, the liquid inside the pot must be brought to a boil with the lid locked in place. When the liquid boils, steam is produced, pressure is created, and thus foods are cooked. Once the lid is securely locked into place, raise the burner to high heat *. As the pressure builds, the pressure valve will activate according to the features of your Fagor Pressure Cooker.

Once maximum pressure has been reached, stabilize the pressure by lowering the burner slightly and then begin your cooking time. Do not lower the burner heat too much, otherwise the internal temperature of the pressure will drop, and the steam and pressure will decrease, not allowing the unit to maintain the desired level of cooking pressure.

*note to electric stove users:

Since the coils on an electric stove retain heat for a long time, food often becomes overcooked when the burner is turned down for simmering (when cooking time is started). To compensate for that, two electric burners should be turned on – one on high heat to bring the cooker to pressure, and the other for simmering so the cooker can be moved over and the cooking time started.

How do I time my recipes?

The amount of time you cook foods is important to achieving the best results, therefore we recommend you have a kitchen timer on hand. Once the desired level of cooking pressure has been reached, set your timer, lower your burner, and begin your cooking time. Because overcooked food cannot be corrected, it is better to cook unfamiliar foods for a shorter period of time than you think is necessary. You can always go back and cook foods a little longer until the desired doneness is reached. You will also note that some recipes have various ingredients that are added during different pressure cooking stages. We recommended that you first add the ingredients that require more time to cook, release the pressure in the cooker, add the remaining ingredients, bring to pressure again, and finish your cooking time by lowering your burner.

What about cooking at High Altitudes?

If you are cooking at a high altitude, the cooking times must be longer, as water and cooking liquids come to a boil more slowly. A rule of thumb to remember is to increase the cooking time by 5% for every 1,000 feet above the first 2,000 feet (3,000 feet above sea level, add 5% to cooking time; 4,000 feet, add 10%; and so on).Since the cooking times increase at altitudes higher than 2,000 feet, you will also have to add more cooking liquid to compensate. There are no fixed rules, so try increasing the cooking liquid by approximately half the percentage of the additional cooking time. For example, if the cooking time is increased by 10%, increase the cooking liquid by 5%.

How Do I Release Pressure?

When the food has finished cooking, remove the pressure cooker from the burner. Although you are no longer cooking, the heat inside the cooker is very hot and foods will continue to cook until the temperature is lowered and the pressure is released. Many of the recipes in this book call for the **Automatic Release Method**, which depressurizes the cooker by turning the valve to the release position. This allows for an instant release of pressure. There are two other methods of releasing pressure from your cooker used in this book. They are:

Natural Release Method:

To use this method, remove the pressure cooker from the hot burner and let the pressure drop and dissipate naturally. Depending on the amount of food and liquid in the pressure cooker, this method can take from 10 to 15 minutes. Open the pressure cooker once the pressure indicator goes down and all the pressure has dissipated.

Quick Release Method:

This is used to release pressure as quickly as possible, as is desired when cooking most vegetables, seafood and other tender foods that can be quickly overcooked. To use this method, remove the pressure cooker from the burner, placing it in the sink and running cold tap water over the lid until steam dissipates and the pressure indicator is lowered. When putting the cooker in the sink, tilt it so the cold water will run downwards. Open the pressure cooker once all of the pressure has been totally released and no additional steam comes out of the operating valve.

Opening the Pressure Cooker:

On all Fagor Pressure Cooker models, the pressure cooker can only be opened after all the built-up pressure has been released. As a safety feature, U.L. (Underwriters Laboratories) now requires that all units have a safety lock that prevents the cooker from being opened until there is no more pressure inside. Since the food in the pressure cooker is extremely hot, use caution in opening and removing the lid. Hold the grip-like handle on the pot with one hand and turn the lid counterclockwise by grasping and turning the lid. Even though the unit is no longer under pressure, there will be some steam rising out and the food will be hot. Therefore, to avoid being burned, never hold your face over the pressure cooker as you remove the lid. In the event you are unable to open the lid, repeat the cold-water release method, as there still may be some remaining pressure in the unit.

How should I wash and store the pressure cooker?

As the Fagor Pressure Cooker is constructed of 18/10 stainless steel with a beautiful mirror finish on the exterior, it should be cleaned and maintained like any other piece of quality cookware.
After each use, wash the inside and outside of the pot and lid with mild dishwashing soap and a non-abrasive sponge, then rinse well. Never fully immerse the lid in water, since it may affect and damage the safety valves. Never wash the lid or gasket in the dishwasher as this could damage the parts and dry out the gasket. When washing the lid, always remove the gasket. Wash the gasket with water and mild dishwashing soap. After washing, towel dry all of the parts of the pressure cooker. Reposition the clean and dried gasket into the lid, under the rim.

IMPORTANT: When storing the pressure cooker, never lock the lid in place, since you can damage the gasket, or worse yet, not be able to reopen the pressure cooker – moisture that may develop can create an almost permanent seal. Always store the lid upside down on top of the pot.

Help is but a phone call away:

If you should have questions, please telephone the Fagor Customer Service Department at 1-800-207-0806 or e-mail us your question at info@fagoramerica.com. Shop Online for Parts & Accessories at: www.fagoramerica.com

Acknowledgments

Fagor America would like to thank Mary Jane Swenson for her contributions to this book. It contains over 50 of her original recipes combined with existing recipes from Fagor's extensive recipe database.

Mary Jane Swenson has been a home economist for over 25 years with a degree from Cal Poly in San Luis Obispo, California. An avid cook and baker, she has taught cooking to both adults and children in the various kitchen arts.

In addition to cooking, she has taught cake decorating since 1991. As a busy wife, mother of two and volunteer, she's learned that delicious food can be fast and easy to prepare using a pressure cooker.

Introduction by Mary Jane Swenson

There are no two words that cause more apprehension for the novice cook than "Pressure Cooker." The mere mention of a pressure cooker will cause many cooks to comment how afraid they are to use one, or about the mishap 40 years ago in their mother's kitchen. There are as many tales as there are cooks. That's history. Today's pressure cookers are safe, simple to use and an essential tool for any busy cook.

I was reintroduced to the pressure cooker a few years ago, and quickly realized that I could reduce my time in the kitchen and still enjoy many favorite dishes. My first experience was making risotto. If you use your pressure cooker only to prepare risotto, you will save countless hours of stirring and hoping for the best, when seven minutes is all you need. Fagor's never fail risotto works every time, you do have to follow the directions, of course. It has become a staple in our house.

The use of a pressure cooker affords you the freedom from relying on many canned or prepackaged foods. High sodium canned beans can be eliminated from your shopping list and replaced with the easy, healthier option of home prepared. In less than 20 minutes dried pinto beans can be transformed into creamy fat free 'refried beans', and that is faster than going to the market and back. Most of the preparation time is waiting for the beans to cook, which is time that can be used to prepare the rest of the meal.

With two very busy teenagers, fast healthy dinners are essential for our family. About 75 per cent of our dinners have at least one ore two dishes prepared in the pressure cooker. I currently have 2 different sizes of cookers and often use both in one meal. Last night dinner was Saltimboca in one cooker and steamed potatoes in the other plus a salad- dinner on the table in less than 30 minutes. A pantry stocked with a few essential items plus your choice of meats will result in meals that will please everyone.

Desserts can also be made in the pressure cooker. Try the flour-less white chocolate cake with raspberry sauce to impress or the various fruit compotes for lighter options. Both will please the palate and many are 'do ahead' recipes so the cooker is available for another part of the meal. In this cookbook you will find a variety of recipes from the simple to a bit more complicated, and many with less than 10 minutes of preparation. Explore the wonderful possibilities of what can be prepared in a single pot, under a bit of heat and pressure, just as coal becomes a diamond under heat and pressure. You might just find a 'diamond' or two in this book that will become standards in you home as they have in mine.

Happy 'pressure' cooking,

Mary Jane Swenson

seafood

Ideally fresh fish should be cooked the day it is bought. If you are defrosting frozen fish, the best way is to place fish in the bottom of the refrigerator for several hours or overnight.

If you don't have time to defrost, frozen fish fillets and shellfish can be also be cooked in the pressure cooker.

When pressure cooking frozen fish, there will be twice as much liquid in the cooker at the end of the cooking time.

The liquid left at the end of pressure cooking can be frozen and used as the basis for fish stock.

Steaming fresh fish in a pressure cooker leaves fish tender and moist. Whether served in a stew or along with rice and/or vegetables, a seafood dish made in a pressure cooker is an excellent choice for a nutritious and easy-to-cook meal.

Steamed Salmon Fillets

Ingredients

1 1/4 pounds salmon fillet
1 large onion, sliced
2 large lemons, sliced
2 gloves of garlic, minced
1/2 cup white wine
Salt and pepper
1 teaspoon dill
2 tablespoons brown sugar

Directions

1   In the pressure cooker place the onions, lemon, garlic and white wine. Lay the salmon on top, skin side down.

2   Season with salt and pepper. Sprinkle on the dill and sugar. Lock the lid in place, bring to high pressure.

3   Stabilize the pressure and cook for 7-9 minutes. Thick fillets may take longer to cook. Release the pressure.

4   Transfer to a platter and serve.

Serves 4

Pressure Cooking Time

7-9 minutes

Marmitako
(Fresh Tuna, Potato, and Green Pepper Stew, Basque Style)

Ingredients

2 tablespoons olive oil

1 medium onion, chopped

1 green bell pepper, cut into strips

3 large baking potatoes, peeled and cut into bite-sized chunks

2 tablespoons paprika

3 cups water

1 pound fresh tuna, cut into small chunks, sprinkled with one teaspoon salt

Serves 6

Pressure Cooking Time

6 minutes

Directions

1   In the pressure cooker, heat the olive oil over medium heat. Sauté the onion for about 3 minutes, just until it begins to soften. Add the green pepper and cook for another 3 minutes. Add the potatoes and paprika; mix well. Cover with 3 cups water.

2   Position lid and lock in place. Raise the heat on stove to high and bring to high pressure. Lower the heat, stabilizing the pressure and cook for 6 minutes.

3   Transfer the pressure cooker to the sink and release the pressure using the cold-water release method. Open the pressure cooker and place it back on the stove.

4   Salt the tuna and add it to the pressure cooker. Over medium-high heat, cook for 2 more minutes, stirring well until the tuna is opaque but not overcooked. Serve in bowls.

Fresh Steamed Lobster

Ingredients

4 cups water
1 1-1/2 pound lobster
Seaweed (optional)
Seasoning (optional)

Directions

1 Put 4 cups of water in a 6 quart or larger pressure cooker.

2 Add seaweed and seasoning to the bottom of
   the cooker (if desired), then place lobster on top
   of seaweed.

3 Close cooker and bring to high pressure, stabilize
   pressure and cook lobster for 3 minutes.

4 When cooking time is up, release pressure using cold-
   water release method.

5 Open cooker, and enjoy!

Serves 1

Pressure Cooking Time

3 minutes

Lobster Risotto

Ingredients

3 tablespoons unsalted butter
1 small onion, finely chopped
1 cup Arborio (short-grain) rice
1/4 cup dry white wine
2 cups low sodium chicken stock, heated
1 medium tomato, peeled, seeded and diced
1/3 cup Parmesan cheese
1/2 cup lobster meat
Freshly ground pepper, to taste
Basil, as garnish

5   Stir in remaining one tablespoon of butter and add
Parmesan cheese. Season with pepper and basil. Stir
thoroughly until all ingredients are blended.

Serves 4

Pressure Cooking Time
7 minutes

Directions

1   In pressure cooker without lid on, heat chicken broth
until hot. Remove from cooker and place in separate
bowl, set aside and keep warm.

2   Heat two tablespoons of unsalted butter in pressure
cooker over medium heat. Add onion and sauté until
translucent. Stir frequently to prevent browning.

3   Add rice and sauté 3 minutes. Add wine and cook,
stirring, for one minute. Add chicken stock, tomatoes
and lobster meat.

4   Put lid in place. Raise heat and set pressure on high.
Once maximum pressure has been reached, stabilize
pressure and cook for 7 minutes. Remove from heat
and release pressure. Open lid.

Oriental Sweet & Sour Shrimp

Ingredients

1 pound small shrimp, peeled
1/4 pound snow peas
3 tablespoons soy sauce
2 tablespoons white vinegar
1/2 cup pineapple juice
2 tablespoons sugar
1 cup chicken broth

Directions

1   In pressure cooker, combine all ingredients. Close lid,
    stabilize pressure and cook 3 minutes.

2   Remove cooker from heat and release pressure. If
    sauce needs to be thickened, place back on stove and
    turn heat on low and stir constantly for a few minutes.

3   Serve hot over rice.

Serves 4

Pressure Cooking Time

3 minutes

Tuna with Pepper Sauce

This wonderful red sauce can be used over any flavorful fish.

Ingredients

3 dried red peppers, mild
2 red peppers for roasting
2 pounds tuna steak
2 medium onions, diced
2 green peppers, diced
1 pound ripe red tomatoes, diced
1/3 cup olive oil
1/8 teaspoon thyme
1/8 teaspoon ground cumin
salt and pepper

Directions

1   Soak the dried peppers in warm water. When they are soft, remove all seeds and scrape the pulp with a spoon. Set aside.

2   Roast the red peppers, peel, and cut in strips. Set aside.

3   Cut the tuna into 8 individual steaks. Heat the oil in the pressure cooker. Gently sauté the diced onion and green peppers seasoned with salt for 10 minutes over medium heat. Add the pulp from the dried red peppers, roasted red pepper strips, diced tomatoes, thyme and cumin.

4   Season the pieces of tuna with salt and pepper and add them to the cooker. Cover, lock lid in place and bring to high pressure. Stabilize pressure and cook for 2 minutes. Release the pressure. Serve the tuna steaks with the sauce.

Serves 6-8

Pressure Cooking Time
2 minutes

Shrimp in a Curried Risotto

Ingredients

1 pound shrimp
1 tablespoon of curry powder
1 large onion
5 cups shrimp stock
3 ribs of celery
1 cup dry white wine
1 red bell pepper
1 cup frozen green peas
3 tablespoons of Spanish olive oil
Salt and pepper to taste
2 cups of Arborio rice

Directions

1 Peel and devein shrimp. Place shrimp back in refrigerator. Reserve shrimp shells for shrimp stock.

2 Dice onion and celery ribs. Remove seeds and ribs from red bell pepper and dice.

3 Make shrimp stock (see *directions*)

4 In pressure cooker pot, sauté onions, red bell pepper and celery in 3 tablespoons of olive oil. When onions are transparent, add Arborio rice and sauté until rice becomes opaque.

5 Stir in curry powder. Add shrimp stock and wine. Close lid, bring to high pressure, then lower heat and cook for 10 minutes.

6 Release pressure using automatic or cold-water release method.

7 Open lid, stir in shrimp meat and green peas and cook for 3-5 minutes until shrimp turn pink. Add salt and pepper to taste.

To Make Shrimp Stock:

Boil shrimp shells in 5 cups of water for 5 minutes. The stock should take on a pink color. Strain shells from stock and discard shells. Retain stock for risotto.

Serves 4

Pressure Cooking Time

10 minutes

Salmon Marinated in Raspberry Sauce
with Aromatic Herbs

Ingredients

4 salmon steaks (1 inch thick)
2 tablespoons fresh lemon juice
1 pint raspberry vinegar (see directions)
1 teaspoon sherry
2 tablespoons olive oil
1 teaspoon salt
4 leeks, cut into 1/2 inch slices
1/4 teaspoon white pepper
2 garlic cloves, crushed
1/3 cup chopped fresh dill
2 tablespoons minced fresh parsley
Fresh raspberries
1 cup bottled clam juice

Directions

1   Marinate salmon steaks in raspberry vinegar, cover
    them and refrigerate them for at least 2 hours.

2   Heat oil in pressure cooker. Add leeks, garlic and
    parsley and sauté in hot oil for 2 minutes. Add clam
    juice, lemon juice, sherry, salt, pepper and dill; stir well.
    Remove salmon steaks from raspberry vinegar
    marinade and place in cooking liquid.

3   Close lid, bring to high pressure, stabilize and cook for
    3 minutes. Release pressure using automatic or cold-
    water release method.

4   Transfer salmon steaks to serving platter. Arrange
    leeks around steaks and garnish with fresh raspberries.

Raspberry Vinegar:

In large stainless steel pan, place 2 pints ripe red
raspberries. Cover them with one pint cider vinegar. Let
stand in cool place for 3 days. Strain liquid and store in
sterile, well-corked glass bottle. Note: Raspberry vinegar
can also be found in select grocery stores.

Serves 4

Pressure Cooking Time
3 minutes

Bouillabaisse

Ingredients

1 pound Hearty fish fillets, cut into chunks
1 pound Lobster tail, cut into chunks
12 oz Scallops
1/4 pound Shrimp
6 clams in shells
4 cups water
3 tablespoons olive oil
2 onions, chopped
2 cloves garlic
2 tablespoons parsley, chopped
1 bay leaf
1 teaspoon thyme
1/4 teaspoon saffron (optional)
Salt and pepper to taste

Serves 4

Pressure Cooking Time

5 minutes + 3 minutes

Directions

1 Heat oil in pressure cooker and sauté onion. Add garlic, parsley, tomatoes, bay leaf, thyme, water, salt and pepper.

2 Close lid, bring to pressure and cook for 5 minutes. Release pressure, open lid and add fish and seafood.

3 Stir. Close lid, bring back up to pressure and cook for 3 minutes. Release pressure, open lid and remove bay leaf. Serve hot.

Salmon with Spinach & Lemon Sauce

Ingredients

1 cup water
1 cup bottled clam juice
1 1/2 teaspoons salt, divided
1/4 cup fresh lemon juice
2 packages (10-ounces each) fresh
1/4 teaspoon white pepper spinach, rinsed and leaves halved
1-1/2 teaspoons dried crumbled dill
2 tablespoons olive oil
6 6-8 ounce each Salmon Steaks
1 medium onion, peeled and halved (at least 1-inch thick)
2 garlic cloves, minced
2 large egg yolks
2 tablespoons minced, fresh broad-leaf parsley
1 teaspoon cornstarch

Directions

1   Pour water into pressure cooker. Stir in 1 teaspoon salt. Place spinach leaves in center of cooker, away from edges.

2   Secure lid and bring to high pressure, then lower heat and cook for 3 minutes.

3   Release pressure using cold-water method and remove the lid.

4   Stir spinach thoroughly; drain through a colander and place on a warm platter, covered; keep warm in a low temperature oven. Wipe moisture from pressure cooker.

5   Heat oil in pressure cooker and add onion, garlic and parsley; sauté in hot oil for 2 minutes.

6   Stir in clam juice, lemon juice and remaining 1/2 teaspoon salt, pepper and dill. Place salmon in cooking liquid; secure lid.

7   Bring up to high pressure, then lower heat and cook for 3 minutes.

8   Release pressure using the cold-water method. Remove lid.

9   Using a slotted spatula, transfer salmon to a platter and cover to retain heat; pour off all but 1/3 cup cooking liquid.

10 Stir egg yolks into remaining liquid. Dissolve cornstarch in a tablespoonful of water and stir into mixture until it begins to thicken.

11 Remove from heat.

12 To serve, arrange a portion of spinach on each of 6 individual plates. Top each with a salmon steak and spoon sauce over salmon. Garnish with sprigs of fresh parsley or thin lemon slices.

Serves 6

Pressure Cooking Time

3 minutes + 3 minutes

Swordfish Teriyaki

The teriyaki marinade creates a flavorful, light, and cholesterol free meal. Serve with white rice.

Ingredients

1 1/2-1 3/4 pounds swordfish or tuna steaks,
   cut in 1 1/2 inch cubes
2 red peppers, cut in 1 1/2 inch pieces
10 scallions, in 1 1/2 inch lengths- thicker portions only
2 tablespoons oil

Teriyaki Sauce:

1/2 cup soy sauce
2 tablespoons sugar
2 tablespoons dry sherry
1 tablespoon rice wine or other white wine
1 1/2 teaspoons grated fresh ginger
2 cloves garlic, minced
1 tablespoon sesame oil
1 teaspoon hoisin sauce

Directions

1 In a large bowl, mix together the fish, peppers, scallions and Teriyaki Sauce ingredients. Marinate for about 30 minutes. Drain and dry on paper towels, reserving the marinade.

2 Heat the oil in the Cooker until very hot.

3 Quickly sauté the scallions and peppers a few seconds and transfer to the Steamer Basket. Sear the fish very briefly and reserve.

4 Pour the marinade into the Cooker and lower the Steamer Basket. Close the lid and bring to pressure. Cook for 1 minute. Release pressure and remove the lid.

5 Add the reserved fish to the Steamer Basket, close the lid and bring to pressure again. Cook for 2 minutes. Release pressure, remove the lid and serve immediately.

Serves 1
Pressure Cooking Time

1 minute + 2 minutes

Squid in it's Ink

To save time, frozen cleaned squid and packets of squid ink are available at most Hispanic markets. Serve with molds of white rice and a green salad for color contrast.

Ingredients

3 pounds squid and it's ink
1 tablespoon of brandy
1/4 cup olive oil
2 large onions, diced
1 clove of garlic, diced
3 tablespoons minced parsley
salt and pepper
3 tablespoons of flour
1 cup dry white wine
1/4 cup tomato paste

Directions

1　Clean the squid and reserve the ink in a small cup with the brandy. Cut the squid in pieces. Put the squid in the pressure cooker with 3 cups of water. Cover, lock lid in place and bring to high pressure.

2　Stabilize pressure and cook for 7 minutes. Release the pressure. Drain the squid. Reserve both the cooking liquid and the squid separately for later. Heat the oil in the cooker over medium heat.

3　Sauté the chopped onion, minced garlic, and parsley that has been seasoned with salt and pepper. Cook until the onions are caramelized.

4　Stir in the flour, reserved ink and the cooking liquid. Cover, lock lid in place and bring to high pressure. Stabilize pressure and cook for 5 minutes.

5　Release the pressure. Puree the ink sauce in a blender. Stir in wine and tomato paste.

6　Place the squid in a saucepan and cover with the sauce. Season with salt and cook for 5 minutes, stirring frequently since it is very prone to sticking.

Serves 4

Pressure Cooking Time
7 minutes + 5 minutes

Stuffed Squid

Gourmet squid for company. Your guests will be delighted!

Ingredients

3 pounds of squid, cleaned.

Stuffing:

1/4 pound prosciutto
1 small onion
2 egg whites, hard boiled
2 garlic cloves, minced
3 tablespoons olive oil
1/4 cup seasoned bread crumbs
1/2 cup flour
1 teaspoon salt
1/2 teaspoon pepper

Sauce:

1/4 cup olive oil
1 large onion, finely diced
2 leeks, (white part only) in thin julienne slices
1 clove of garlic
2 tablespoons minced parsley
1/2 cup white wine
salt to taste
2 egg yolks, hard boiled
6 unblanched almonds

Directions

1   Clean the squid and set aside the tubes.

2   To prepare the stuffing, heat the 3 tablespoons of oil in a skillet and sauté the onion and garlic over low heat until very soft. Add the diced ham and the finely minced egg whites. Sauté for a few minutes.

3   Using a small spoon, stuff the squid and close the opening with a toothpick. Combine the flour, salt and pepper in a small bowl. Dredge the stuffed squid in the seasoned flour.

4   Heat the 1/4 cup of oil in the pressure cooker and sauté the stuffed squid until lightly golden. Remove from the pan and set aside.

5   In the same oil, lightly sauté the finely diced onion, leeks and the garlic clove until a light golden color. Season with salt. Add the minced parsley, white wine, 1/2 cup of water and the squid. Cover, lock lid in place and bring to high pressure.

6   Stabilize pressure and cook for 7 minutes. Let cool gradually. Remove the squid to a casserole, set aside and keep warm.

7   In a blender puree the sauce with the egg yolks and blanched almonds. Pour over the stuffed squid and gently bring to a gentle boil stirring constantly. Check seasonings and serve.

Serves 6

Pressure Cooking Time

7 minutes

Stuffed Hake or Sea Bass Tail

This is a lovely presentation that takes some effort, but well worth it. An alternate presentation is to prepare the tail by opening it like a book and closing it well after stuffing.

Ingredients

3 pounds fresh hake or sea bass tail
5 tablespoons olive oil, divided
2 potatoes, peeled and thinly sliced
1 medium onion, finely diced
1 clove garlic, minced
6 oz fresh shrimp, peeled and coarsely chopped
3 slices of Serrano ham or prosciutto, diced
6 oz fresh mushrooms, chopped
1 tablespoon of minced parsley
2 tablespoon flour mixed with 1 tablespoon water
   to form a paste
juice of 1 orange
1 cup water
1/2 cup bread crumbs
salt to taste

Directions

1 Scale the fish tail. To remove the main spine, make a cut on the upper end of the tail and gradually introduce a knife with a long, narrow blade, turning the fish to loosen it a bit at a time. When the end has been reached, pull on the spine, which will come out whole. Reserve fish.

2 Grease an ovenproof casserole with 1 tablespoon oil, layer the sliced potatoes, season with salt, and bake at 350° F until golden, about 20 minutes. Keep warm.

3 Meanwhile, heat 2 tablespoons of oil in a skillet and sauté the diced onion, garlic, shrimp, ham and the mushrooms. When the water from the mushrooms has evaporated, sprinkle on the minced parsley. Let cool.

4 Fill the fish tail using a long handled spoon so you can reach the very tip of the tail. Plug the opening with the paste made from water and flour.

5 Place 1 cup water, 2 tablespoons oil, and a pinch of salt in the pressure cooker. Position a steamer basket and place the stuffed fish in the basket.

6 Sprinkle with orange juice. Cover, lock lid in place and bring to high pressure. Stabilize pressure and cook for 7 minutes. Release the pressure.

7 Place the steamed fish on top of the prepared potatoes. Sprinkle with the bread crumbs and bake at 500° F until crumbs are golden. Serve.

Serves 6

Pressure Cooking Time
7 minutes

Grouper Salad

For a finished presentation, serve on a bed of finely shredded lettuce and sliced cooked potatoes. The potatoes, unpeeled, can be cooked at the same time as the fish.

Ingredients

2 pounds grouper or sea bass steaks, skin
   and bones removed
salt and pepper
4 anchovies packed in olive oil
1 teaspoon prepared mustard
3 drops of Tabasco
1 tomato, peeled and diced
1 small sweet onion, chopped
2/3 cup virgin olive oil
1 tablespoon of sweet paprika
1 lemon, cut in half
2 avocados
salt

Directions

1   If frozen, thaw the fish. Season both sides with salt and pepper. Put 2 cups of water in the pressure cooker, position the steamer basket in the cooker, and place the fish in the basket. Cover, lock lid in place and bring to high pressure. Stabilize pressure and cook for 3 minutes. Release the pressure using the cold-water release method. Remove the fish to a platter and chill. When cold, cut the fish into 1/2 inch slices.

2   Make the vinaigrette. In a food processor or blender, puree the anchovies, prepared mustard, Tabasco, tomato, sweet onion, oil, juice of 1/2 lemon and the sweet paprika until smooth. Adjust the salt and pepper if necessary. Chill.

3   Peel the avocados, remove the pits, and cut into thin slices. Arrange them in the shape of a wheel on a platter and sprinkle with the juice of half a lemon. Place the slices of fish on top of the avocado slices, and dress with some of the vinaigrette. Serve the remaining sauce on the side.

Serves 6

Pressure Cooking Time
3 minutes

Jumbo Shrimp with Saffron Rice

This recipe can easily be doubled or tripled for a crowd.

Ingredients

1 1/4 pounds Jumbo Shrimp
juice of 1 lemon, divided
2 garlic cloves, minced
1 teaspoon sweet paprika, divided
1 teaspoon hot paprika, divided
1/3 cup olive oil
1 1/2 cups Arborio rice
1 ripe firm tomato, peeled and diced
1/4 teaspoon saffron threads
2 cup hot fish stock or chicken stock
salt to taste

Directions

1   Peel and devein the shrimp, leaving the tails on. Place them in a bowl. Combine 1 minced garlic clove, 1/2 teaspoon of hot paprika, 1/2 teaspoon of sweet paprika, 2 tablespoons of olive oil, pinch of salt and the juice of 1/2 lemon. Pour over the shrimp and set aside.

2   Heat the remaining oil in the pressure cooker over medium heat. Gently saute the tomato with the other clove of garlic. Season with salt. When the tomato is cooked, add the rice and cook slowly for 2 minutes, stirring with a wooden spoon. Add the remaining hot and mild paprika, and the saffron threads.

3   Stir rapidly and pour in 2 cups of hot stock. Add the juice of the remaining lemon half. Cover, lock lid in place and bring to high pressure. Stabilize pressure and cook for 8 minutes. Release the pressure.

4   While the rice is cooking, quickly sauté the marinated shrimp in a hot skillet. Press the cooked rice in a crown-shaped mold and unmold quickly. (if you don't have a mold you can use a bowl)

5   Serve garnished with the cooked shrimp arranged on top

Serves 4

Pressure Cooking Time
8 minutes

Warm Tuna Salad

Serve this salad over a bed of shredded Napa cabbage.

Ingredients

4 tablespoons olive oil, divided
2 large carrots, sliced lengthwise in very thin strips
2 large zucchini, sliced lengthwise in very thin strips
1 pound tuna steak
3 onions cut into thin wedges
2 cloves garlic, minced
1 teaspoon fresh ginger, peeled and minced
1 cup white wine
1/4 cup rice vinegar
4 black peppercorns
salt and pepper

Directions

1   Heat 2 tablespoons of the olive oil in the pressure cooker over medium heat and sauté the strips of carrot and zucchini. Season lightly with salt. Remove from the cooker and set aside. Keep warm.

2   Season the tuna steak on both sides with salt and pepper. Heat the remaining oil in the pressure cooker over medium heat and gently sauté the onions, garlic, minced ginger and the peppercorns.

3   Place the tuna steak on top of the onions. Pour in the vinegar and white wine. Cover, lock lid in place and bring to high pressure. Stabilize pressure and cook for 3 minutes. Release pressure.

4   Take the tuna steak of the pressure cooker. Cut in pieces, arrange the pieces on a platter. Cook the sauce with the lid off for a few minutes to thicken it.

5   Serve the tuna steak still warm, accompanied by the vegetables. and dressed with the sauce

Serves 4

Pressure Cooking Time
3 minutes

Grouper with Sea Urchin Sauce

Minced mussels or crushed anchovies in oil may be used in place of the preserved sea urchin caviar. For a more delicate and less salty version use fresh sea urchin caviar available at most Asian markets.

Ingredients

2 pounds firm white fish (grouper, sea bass, etc).
3 cups water
1 cup of fish broth
1/2 cup of dry white wine
1 teaspoon of sage
1 teaspoon of dill
salt to taste
1 tablespoon butter
1 tablespoon olive oil
2 tablespoons of grated onion
2 cloves garlic, minced
1 level tablespoon of corn starch
1 tin of sea urchin caviar
2 tablespoons minced parsley

Directions

1 Combine 3 cups of water, fish broth, wine, sage, the dill, and 1 teaspoon of salt in the pressure cooker. Place the grouper in a steamer basket in the cooker. Cover, lock lid in place and bring to high pressure. Stabilize pressure and cook for 3 minutes. Release the pressure. Remove one cup of broth from the cooker and set aside. Leave the fish on the basket inside the cooker to keep it hot.

2 In a skillet over low heat, add the butter and olive oil. Gently sauté the grated onion and the minced garlic. Season with a pinch of salt if desired. Combine the corn starch with the reserved fish broth and stir.

3 Keeping the heat low, add the cornstarch mixture to the onions, stir until the sauce becomes thickened and translucent. Add the contents of the sea urchin caviar and continue to stir constantly.

4 Serve the fish on 6 plates with the hot sea urchin sauce, sprinkled with a generous pinch of minced parsley.

Serves 6

Pressure Cooking Time
3 minutes

Red Snapper in Green Sauce
with Asparagus and Mushrooms

Ingredients

1/2 cup olive oil

1/2 pound fresh mushrooms, washed and sliced

1 onion, chopped

1 clove of garlic, sliced very thin

2 pounds red snapper

salt and pepper

1 cup flour

2 tablespoons minced parsley

2/3 cup dry white wine

2 cups water or white fish broth

1 dozen asparagus, peeled and cut in 2 inch pieces

Directions

1   Heat 1 tablespoon of oil in the pressure cooker over medium heat and sauté the sliced mushrooms until their liquid evaporates. Remove from the cooker and set aside for later.

2   Heat the remaining oil in the cooker and gently sauté the chopped onion and garlic, over medium heat until the garlic is soft and transparent. Remove the garlic and onions with a slotted spatula. Set aside for later.

3   Cut red snapper in medium sized pieces, and season with salt and pepper. Dredge in the flour, put them in the cooker with the warmed oil. Add the white wine, the fish broth (or water), and the minced parsley. Cover, lock lid in place and bring to high pressure. Stabilize pressure and cook for 2 minutes. Release the pressure.

4   Return the cooker to medium heat and add the reserves mushrooms, onions, garlic and asparagus. Cook the stew for a few minutes, stirring constantly until the asparagus are bright green and tender crisp. Add salt and pepper to taste.

5   Serve garnished with a sprinkling of sweet paprika.

Serves 6

Pressure Cooking Time

2 minutes

Fresh Cod Timbale

A casserole that is reminiscent of fish and chips.

Ingredients

1/2 pound fresh cod fillet, remove skin and bones
1/2 pound potatoes, peeled and cut into 1 inch cubes
1 teaspoon salt
1 whole egg
1 egg, separated
1 onion, diced
1 clove garlic, minced
2 tablespoons olive oil
2 tablespoons ketchup
1 tablespoon mustard
1 teaspoon thyme
grated nutmeg
2 tablespoons butter
1/4 cup seasoned bread crumbs

Directions

1 Place the potatoes and cod in the pressure cooker with 1 cup of water and salt. Lock the lid in place, bring to high pressure. Stabilize the pressure and cook for 5 minutes. Release the pressure. Drain the potatoes and fish and set aside.

2 Heat the oil in a skillet over medium heat and sauté the onion and garlic until the onion is transparent. Remove from the heat and place in a mixing bowl. Add the drained potato and fish mixture, mustard, ketchup, thyme, whole egg and the extra egg yolk.

3 Mix until well combined. In a separate bowl, beat the egg white until stiff peaks form. Fold the egg white into the fish mixture.

4 Grease a pressure cooker baking dish with butter and sprinkle with bread crumbs. Shake out any excess bread crumbs. Fill with the fish mixture. Sprinkle with freshly grated nutmeg. Cover with aluminum foil. Place the baking dish on a trivet in the bottom of the pressure cooker with at least 1 inch of water. Try not to have the water touching the base of the baking dish. Cover, lock lid in place and bring to high pressure. Stabilize pressure and cook for 15 minutes. Release the pressure.

Serves 4

Pressure Cooking Time
5 minutes + 15 minutes

Stewed Octopus in Casserole

Grouper or sea bass can be used instead of octopus. Add it to the stew once the potatoes and clams have been cooked.

Ingredients

1 pound baby octopus prepared. See instructions
1 1/2 pounds clams
2 large onions, chopped finely
2 cloves of garlic, minced
1/2 teaspoon salt
4 medium potatoes, peeled and cut into 1 inch cubes
2 tablespoons of sweet paprika
1⁄2 teaspoon of hot paprika
1 cup dry white wine
1/4 cup olive oil
1 cup water

Directions

1 Cook the baby octopus the day before, following the instructions in the Galician-style octopus. (See recipe on page 38).

2 Put the clams in cold water with a splash of vinegar or salt so they will release their grit. Do this at least one hour before cooking.

3 Heat the oil in the pressure cooker and sauté the onions and garlic over medium heat until translucent. Season with salt. Add the potatoes and the sweet and the hot paprika. Simmer for 5 minutes, stirring with a wooden spoon. Pour in the white wine and water.

4 Cover, lock lid in place and bring to high pressure. Stabilize pressure and cook for 2 minutes. Turn off the heat and let the cooker rest for 4 minutes. Release the pressure using quick release method. Open the lid and add the octopus and clams, and continue to cook over medium heat until the clams have opened. Turn off the heat, cover the cooker with a clean cloth and let it sit for 10 minutes before serving.

Serves 4

Pressure Cooking Time
2 minutes

Galician-Style Octopus

Fresh baby octopus is readily available at most fish markets, but you will need to pre order it. They are approximately 1 to 2 ounces each and are already cleaned.

Serves 4

Pressure Cooking Time
10 minutes

Ingredients

1/4 pound fresh baby octopus
virgin olive oil
sweet paprika
hot paprika
coarsely ground sea salt

Directions

1   Wash the octopus thoroughly.

2   Bring 4 cups of water to the boil in the pressure cooker. When the water is boiling, add the octopus to the pot. Cover, lock the lid in place and bring to high pressure. Stabilize pressure and cook for 10 minutes. Release the pressure.

3   Drain the pot and place the octopus in a bowl. Season to taste with sea salt, sweet and hot paprika, and sprinkle liberally with olive oil.

4   Serve immediately.

rice, grains & pasta

A healthy body needs a lot of cooked grain. Whole grain provides the best nutrition possible, with B vitamins and other important nutrients.

Brown rice, millet, wheat and barley are wonderful sources of nutrition. They can be prepared easily and are satisfying to eat.

Buckwheat, corn, oats, spelt and rye are also excellent additions to a healthful diet. Long grain rice varieties, corn and seed-like grains such quinoa also make for wholesome meals.

Pasta is not only a satisfying & very affordable meal, but also, it is a good source of an extremely important vitamin called folic acid - one that helps protect our good health. Pasta is also easy to combine with other folate-rich foods such as vegetables, nuts and fruits.

Kale and Potato Risotto

Ingredients

2 tablespoons olive oil
2 tablespoons butter
2 small onions, chopped
2 medium boiling potatoes, peeled,
    cut into 1/2 inch chunks
1 large kale or 2 small bunches, with leaves chopped
2 cups Arborio rice
1/2 cup white wine
4 1/2 cups low sodium vegetable stock, boiled
1 cup Parmesan cheese
Italian parsley, chopped

Serves 8

Pressure Cooking Time
7 minutes

Directions

1   In pressure cooker, heat oil and butter. Add onions,
    potatoes and kale. Sauté over medium-high heat until
    kale wilts some and onions give off aroma.

2   Add Arborio to warm potato-kale mixture and stir
    briefly, until rice turns opaque, about 1 minute. Add
    wine and stir until evaporated. Add boiling stock,
    close pressure cooker, bring up to high pressure, then
    lower heat and cook for 7 minutes.

3   Release pressure using cold-water release method.
    Open cooker, stir risotto, taste and if necessary, cook
    further to desired consistency.

4   Add Parmesan cheese and parsley and serve immediately.

Winter Squash Risotto

Creamy risotto, a delicious Italian dish, is very time-consuming when using traditional cooking methods. In a pressure cooker, you can achieve wonderful results in a matter of minutes!

Ingredients

- 5 tablespoons unsalted butter
- 1 1/2 cups diced peeled butternut squash
- 1 large onion, chopped
- 3 1/2 cups vegetable broth, warmed
- 1 1/2 cups Arborio rice
- 1/2 cup dry white wine
- 1/4 cup Parmesan cheese
- 1 tablespoon fresh parsley, minced

Directions

1. In pressure cooker pot, melt butter over medium-low heat. Add onion and sauté until tender but not brown, about 2 minutes.

2. Add squash and 1/2 cup broth to onions and stir for an additional minute.

3. Add remaining vegetable broth, rice and white wine. Close lid, bring to high pressure, then lower heat and cook for 7 minutes.

4. Release pressure. Open lid and add Parmesan cheese. Stir thoroughly. Divide evenly among plates, garnish with parsley and serve while very hot.

Serves 4

Pressure Cooking Time
7 minutes

Risotto with Peas

This wonderful Mediterranean dish once took a long time to make. Now it is easy in a pressure cooker.

Ingredients

3 tablespoons butter
1 small onion, finely chopped
1 cup Arborio or other short-grain rice
1 cup frozen peas
2 1/4 cups chicken broth
1/3 cup Parmesan cheese
1/8 teaspoon pepper

Serves 4

Pressure Cooking Time
7 minutes

Directions

1   In cooker, heat 2 tablespoons of butter over medium heat. Sauté onion in butter for 4-5 minutes, until soft. Stir frequently so onion does not brown. Add rice, and sauté until light brown. Add peas and chicken stock; stir well. Close lid and bring to pressure. Lower heat and cook for 7 minutes.

2   Release pressure and open the lid. Stir in additional one tablespoon of butter, Parmesan and pepper. Let sit until butter and cheese melts. Stir thoroughly and serve.

Rice Pilaf

Pine nuts and raisins give this rice a distinctive Middle Eastern flavor.

Ingredients

2 tablespoons butter
2 tablespoons minced onion
1 cup rice
2 cups chicken stock
2 tablespoons pine nuts
2 tablespoons golden raisins
1 teaspoon thyme
1 tablespoon minced parsley
Salt and freshly ground pepper

Directions

1. Melt the butter in the Cooker and sauté the onion until softened. Add the rice and coat it with the butter. Add the remaining ingredients and bring to a boil.

2. Close the lid and bring to pressure. Lower heat and cook for 3 minutes. Release pressure, open cooker and drain off any excess liquid. Dry in oven before serving.

Serves 4

Pressure Cooking Time

3 minutes

Paella, Spanish Style

Here is a simple version of a seafood Paella that you can prepare in your cooker in no time. If you wish to make the popular mixed seafood and meat version, add chicken, cut in small serving portions and sliced chorizo or other sausage.

Ingredients

8 small mussels or clams (cleaned)
2 tablespoons olive oil
1/2 pound firm white fish, such as monkfish, halibut or scrod, cut in 1 inch pieces
1/2 pound shrimp, shelled
1 medium onion, chopped
3 cloves garlic, minced
1 pimiento, chopped
1 tablespoon minced parsley
1/4 teaspoon paprika
1 small tomato, skinned, seeded and chopped
2 cups rice-short or long grain
4 cups fish stock, clam juice or chicken broth
1/2 cup peas
1 /4 teaspoon saffron

Directions

1   Place 1 cup water in the cooker and bring to a boil. Add the mussels and cook until they open. Discard half of the shell, and reserve the mussels on a warm platter.

2   Dry the cooker thoroughly. Heat the oil until very hot, and sauté the fish and the shrimp until they are just cooked.

3   Transfer to a platter and cover tightly with foil. Add the onion and garlic to the Cooker and sauté until the onion is wilted. Stir in the pimiento, parsley, paprika and then the tomato.

4   Cook 3 minutes. Stir in the rice and coat well. Pour in the stock then add the peas and the saffron and bring to a boil. Close the lid, bring to pressure and cook for 3 minutes. Remove from the flame and let the cooker sit closed for 4 minutes before releasing the pressure.

5   Remove the lid and stir in the reserved mussels, fish and shrimp.

Serves 4

Pressure Cooking Time
3 minutes

Mediterranean Risotto

Ingredients

1 6-1/2 ounce jar artichoke hearts (quartered), drained, reserve liquid/oil
2-3 cloves garlic, peeled and minced
1 cup Arborio rice
2 1/4 cups vegetable stock
8 large stuffed olives
2 roasted red peppers (from jar), drained and patted dry
1/4 cup sliced sun dried tomatoes (either packed in oil or reconstituted in water, drained)
1/4 pound Gruyere cheese, diced
3 tablespoons Italian parsley, chopped
Pepper

Directions

1   Heat 2 tablespoons of artichoke liquid/oil in pressure cooker over medium-high heat. Add garlic and sauté for 30 seconds. Add the rice and sauté, stirring often, until lightly golden. Pour in stock. Stir well.

2   Position the lid and lock in place. Bring to high pressure then lower heat and cook for 7 minutes.

3   While risotto is cooking, slice the olives and roasted red peppers.

4   Remove risotto from heat and release pressure using automatic or cold-water release method. Stir in artichoke hearts, olives, roasted red peppers, sun dried tomatoes, Gruyere cheese, and 1 tablespoon of reserved liquid.

5   Let risotto sit in cooker until cheese has melted. Stir one more time and sprinkle with Italian parsley and pepper. Serve at once.

Serves 4

Pressure Cooking Time
7 minutes

Spanish Risotto

Ingredients

1 teaspoon saffron threads
2 cups low-sodium vegetable broth warmed
1 tablespoon extra-virgin olive oil
3 1/4 cups Rioja wine
3 cloves garlic, minced
5 ounces shallots, trimmed and minced
3/4 cup pitted imported green olives, sliced and divided
2 1/2 cups Arborio rice
4 tablespoons fresh mint, torn

Garnish:
3 ounces Manchego cheese, grated coarsely
   (or substitute with Pecorino cheese)
Parsley oil (see below)

Directions

1   Infuse saffron by placing in warm vegetable broth and set aside.

2   Heat one tablespoon of oil in a 6 quart or larger pressure cooker, then add shallots and garlic. Sauté until translucent, about 2 minutes, then add rice, 4 tablespoons mint, stirring to coat rice.

3   Add the wine, 2 cups of broth with saffron, wine and half the olives.

4   Lock lid in place, bring up to high pressure then cook for 7 minutes.

5   Open cooker using cold-water release method. Stir thoroughly. If necessary, add salt and pepper to taste. The risotto should be very creamy. If not, add 1/4 cup more stock and cook one additional minute without pressure.

6   Ladle portions of risotto into warmed shallow plates. Drizzle each portion with one teaspoon of parsley oil (see below). Garnish with cheese and mint leaves. Serve immediately while hot.

PARSLEY OIL:
1/4 cup extra-virgin Spanish olive oil, warmed
3 tablespoons chopped parsley, coarsely chopped.

7   Warm 1/4 cup olive oil in a small saucepan until hot but not scalding. Transfer to a mini processor or blender and blend with parsley and mint leaves. Strain through a fine strainer into a small jar.

8   You will only need 6 teaspoons for this recipe. Refrigerate remainder for later use.

Serves 6

Pressure Cooking Time
7 minutes

Country Style Potatoes

Ingredients

1 tablespoon olive oil
1/4 pound fresh mushrooms, stems trimmed, sliced
1/2 cup finely chopped onion
1/2 teaspoon salt
1/8 teaspoon pepper
1/2 cup chicken stock or water
4 cups potatoes in 1/2 inch slices
2 tablespoons minced parsley

Directions

1. In the cooker, heat the oil and sauté the mushrooms and onions until the onions are wilted.

2. Mix in all the remaining ingredients.

3. Close the lid and bring to high pressure, then lower heat and cook for 3 minutes.

4. Release pressure and remove the lid. Serve.

Serves 4

Pressure Cooking Time

3 minutes

Orange Rice

Ingredients

1 1/2 cups brown basmati rice
1/2 cup wild rice
2 1/2 cups water
1/8 teaspoon sea salt
1/4 cup fresh squeezed orange juice
1/2 cup dried currants
2 naval oranges
2 tablespoons shelled sunflower seeds (unsalted)
3 tablespoons olive oil
2 tablespoons sweet brown rice vinegar

Directions

1   Place water and brown and wild rice into cooker. With lid on, but not locked, bring to a brisk boil, then add sea salt.

2   Lock cooker and bring to high pressure, then lower heat and cook for 20 minutes. Remove cooker from stove and allow pressure to reduce naturally.

3   While rice is cooking, remove skin from oranges and separate into sections. Heat orange juice and pour on currants to moisten.

4   In a dry saucepan over medium heat, toast sunflower seeds for 3 minutes, stirring frequently. Remove from pan for later use.

5   After pressure has reduced, open and remove lid, adding remaining ingredients except sunflower seeds.

6   Mix well and place in serving dish. Prior to serving, sprinkle with toasted sunflower seeds.

Serves 4

Pressure Cooking Time
20 minutes

Steamed Rice

Ingredients

3 tablespoons olive oil
1 cup long-grain rice
2 cups low sodium chicken broth or water
1 tablespoon butter
Salt and pepper, to taste

Directions

1 Heat oil in pressure cooker. Stir in rice, then add broth
   or water.

2 Close lid, bring up to high pressure, then lower heat
   and cook 8 minutes.

3 Release pressure, open lid, add butter, plus salt
   and pepper to taste. Mix thoroughly. Serve at once
   while hot.

Serves 4

Pressure Cooking Time
8 minutes

Artichoke and Rice Salad

This is a wonderful cold salad for a light meal. To make it more substantial, add 2 cups of diced cooked chicken.

Ingredients

2 tablespoons olive oil
1 cup long grain white rice
2 cups chicken stock
2 jars marinated artichoke hearts
1/4 cup slivered almonds
1/4 cup chopped green onions
1/4 cup diced red bell pepper
1 small can chopped water chestnuts, drained
1/4 cup sliced black olives
3/4 cup mayonnaise
1 tablespoon balsamic vinegar
2 tablespoons chopped flat leaf parsley
Salt and pepper to taste

Directions

1. Heat oil in the pressure cooker. Stir in rice and chicken stock. Close lid, bring to high pressure. Stabilize pressure and cook for 8 minutes. Release pressure and transfer rice to large bowl.

2. Drain artichokes, reserving marinade. Chop artichokes and stir into rice. Combine reserved marinade with mayonnaise and vinegar. Stir into rice along with almonds, green onions, bell pepper, water chestnuts, black olives and parsley. Chill for several hours.

3. Season with salt and pepper, if needed. This tastes best if made one day ahead. Serve with melon slices and rolls.

Serves 4

Pressure Cooking Time

8 minutes

Black and White Rice

This two step process results in a colorful rice that is the perfect accompaniment to almost any dinner. Choose the flavor of broth to complement the main course. This can easily be doubled.

Serves 4

Pressure Cooking Time

18 minutes + 7 minutes

Ingredients

1/3 cup wild rice
3 cups water
1/2 teaspoon salt
1 teaspoon oil
1 cup white rice
1/4 cup minced shallot or onion
2 cup water or broth

Directions

1   Rinse and drain the wild rice. Place the wild rice in the pressure cooker with the 3 cups water and 1/2 teaspoon salt. Lock the lid in place, bring to high pressure. Stabilize the pressure and cook for 18 minutes. The grains will pop open. Release the pressure.

2   Drain the wild rice, set aside and keep warm. Heat the oil in the pressure cooker and stir in the white rice and onion. Sauté for a minute or two. Add the water or broth and salt if desired.

3   Lock the lid in place, bring to high pressure. Stabilize the pressure and cook for 7 minutes. Release the pressure. Stir in the reserved wild rice and serve.

Creamy Corn Casserole

*These simple pantry staples become a wonderful
creamy cornbread.*

Ingredients

butter for greasing
1 14.75 ounce can of cream style corn
1 8.12 ounce box of cornbread mix
1 8 ounce container of nonfat vanilla yogurt
1 egg

Directions

1. Grease a pressure cooker baking dish with butter and
set aside. In a mixing bowl, combine all the ingredients
until just blended. Pour into the prepared dish and
cover tightly with a piece of foil. Place a trivet in the
pressure cooker with water just below the baking dish.

2. Place the filled dish on the trivet. Lock the lid in place,
bring to high pressure. Stabilize the pressure and cook
for 45 minutes. Release the pressure. Carefully remove
the dish from the cooker and serve.

Serves 4

Pressure Cooking Time

45 minutes

Fagor's Never Fail Risotto

Only 7 minutes to perfectly creamy risotto. If you only use you pressure cooker for one dish this is it!

Ingredients

2 tablespoons olive oil
1/4 cup diced onion or shallot
1 cup Arborio rice
2 cups chicken broth
1/4 cup white wine
1 teaspoon saffron threads
1/4 grated Parmesan cheese
1 tablespoon fresh minced parsley

Directions

1. In the pressure cooker, over medium heat, heat the olive oil. Stir in the onion and rice and sauté until the onion is translucent. Add the broth, wine and saffron.

2. Lock the lid in place, bring to high pressure. Stabilize the pressure and cook for 7 minutes. Release the pressure. Stir in the cheese and parsley. Serve.

Serves 4

Pressure Cooking Time
7 minutes

Quick Rich Mushroom Sauce for Pasta

This looks complicated, but really isn't. The dried mushrooms and truffle oil add an intense flavor to the sauce and are well worth the extra effort and expense. A green salad is all that is needed to complete this company worthy dinner.

Ingredients

1 1/2 cups walnut halves
1/2 ounce dried porcini mushrooms
1 cup water
3 tablespoons olive oil
1 1/2 pounds mixed fresh mushrooms sliced
1/2 cup white wine
1/2 cup grated Parmesan cheese
3/4 cup cream
Salt and pepper to taste
Truffle oil (optional)
8 ounces cooked pasta (rotini or bow ties work well)

Directions

1 In a separate pan, bring water to a boil and cook pasta according to package directions.

2 In the pressure cooker, over medium heat, toast the walnut halves until fragrant. Stir frequently so they do not burn. Remove walnuts and set aside. Remove any visible grit for the porcini mushrooms, add them to the cooker along with the 1 cup of water.

3 Lock the lid in place, bring to high pressure. Stabilize the pressure and cook for 7 minutes. Release the pressure. Drain the porcini mushrooms reserving the liquid, it will be about 1/3 of a cup, again check for any grit. Rinse the porcinis to remove any additional grit and chop.

4 In the cooker, heat the olive oil and lightly sauté the sliced fresh mushrooms and porcini. Add the white wine and reserved liquid. Lock the lid in place, bring to high pressure. Stabilize the pressure and cook for and additional 5 minutes. Release the pressure. Slightly reduce the remaining liquid in the pot. Remove from heat and stir in the grated cheese and cream.

5 Season to taste with salt and pepper. Add the prepared pasta noodles and reserved toasted walnuts and toss. Serve with a drizzle of truffle oil if desired.

Serves 4

Pressure Cooking Time

7 minutes + 5 minutes

Breakfast Casserole

Fast, easy and great as a leftover the next day or a light dinner.

Ingredients

- 4 eggs, beaten
- 3/4 cup milk
- 1/4 cup diced cooked bacon or sausage
- 2 tablespoons chopped sun dried tomato
- 1/2 cup grated cheese, Cheddar or Swiss work best
- 5 slices bread, cubed

Serves 4

Pressure Cooking Time
20 minutes

Directions

1. Combine all of the ingredients in a mixing bowl and set aside for the moisture to be absorbed into the bread, about 30 minutes. Generously butter a pressure cooker baking dish.

2. Pour in the bread and egg mixture. Cover tightly with a piece of foil that has been buttered, buttered side facing down to prevent sticking.

3. Place on a trivet in the bottom of the pressure cooker with at least 1 inch of water. Try not to have the water touching the base of the baking dish.

4. Cover, lock lid in place and bring to high pressure. Stabilize pressure and cook for 20 minutes. Release pressure, remove foil and serve.

Cheesy Grits

The flavor of this dish can be varied by the type of cheese used. Use cheddar for a mild choice, but gorgonzola or smoked gouda really pack a flavor punch.

Ingredients

3 cups water
1 cup milk
3/4 cups grits
1 cup grated cheese (your choice)
Salt
Pepper
1 tablespoon minced fresh parsley

Directions

1. In the pressure cooker, bring the milk and water to a boil. Stir in the grits.

2. Lock the lid in place, bring to high pressure. Stabilize the pressure and cook for 7 minutes. Release the pressure. Stir in the grated cheese and parsley.

3. Check seasonings. Add salt and pepper if desired. Certain cheeses will need more seasoning than others. Serve immediately.

Serves 4

Pressure Cooking Time

7 minutes

Orange Quinoa

Ingredients

1/4 cup pecans, roughly chopped

1 cup of quinoa rinsed in cold water and drained

1 tablespoon olive oil

1 teaspoon ginger, minced

1/4 cup diced carrots

2 cups chicken stock

1/4 fresh squeezed orange juice

1/4 cup dried cranberries

Directions

1. In the pressure cooker, over medium heat, lightly toast the pecans and set them aside for later. In the cooker heat the olive oil and stir in the ginger and carrots. Add the rinsed quinoa, chicken stock, orange juice and cranberries.

2. Lock the lid in place, bring to high pressure. Stabilize the pressure and cook for 7 minutes. Release the pressure. Remove the lid. Stir in the reserved toasted pecans. Serve.

Serves 4

Pressure Cooking Time

7 minutes

Quinoa with Broccoli

Quinoa, pronounced "keen-wah", is an important staple of South American cuisine. It has a higher protein content than most grains.

Serves 4

Pressure Cooking Time
7 minutes

Ingredients

- 1/4 cup slivered almonds
- 1 cup of quinoa rinsed in cold water and drained
- 1 tablespoon olive oil
- 1 clove garlic, minced
- 2 cups chicken stock
- 1 teaspoon soy sauce
- 1 cup broccoli florets

Directions

1. In the pressure cooker, over medium heat, lightly toast the almonds and set them aside for later. In the cooker heat the olive oil and stir in the garlic. Add the rinsed quinoa, chicken stock and soy sauce.

2. Lock the lid in place, bring to high pressure. Stabilize the pressure and cook for 7 minutes. Release the pressure. Remove the lid and immediately stir in the broccoli florets.

3. Re-cover the cooker for 4 additional minutes-do not turn on the heat. The residual heat will perfectly cook the broccoli. Stir in the reserved slivered almonds. Serve.

Sweet Breakfast Grits

It's hard to believe that these are humble grits. A great way to start the day.

Ingredients

1/4 cup pecans
3 cups water
1 cup milk
1/4 cup golden raisins
1/4 cup currants
1/4 cup brown sugar
1/2 teaspoons ground cinnamon
1/8 teaspoons freshly ground nutmeg
3/4 cup grits
butter

Serves 4

Pressure Cooking Time
7 minutes

Directions

1. In the pressure cooker, over medium heat, toast the pecan pieces. When done, remove from pan and set aside for later use. In the pressure cooker, combine the milk, water, raisins, currants, spices, sugar and bring to a boil. Stir in the grits.

2. Lock the lid in place, bring to high pressure. Stabilize the pressure and cook for 7 minutes. Release the pressure. Stir in the reserved toasted pecans. Serve immediately with a pat of butter floating on top.

Super Fast Pasta Sauce

In a hurry? This fast sauce will be done before your pasta water has boiled. If desired, stir in a teaspoon of red pepper flakes for a spicy version of this traditional sauce. To be served with the pasta of your choice.

Ingredients

2 tablespoons olive oil
2-3 cloves of garlic, minced
28 ounce can of ground tomatoes
1 teaspoon sugar
1/4 teaspoon dried oregano
1 tablespoon prepared pesto

1/2 pound of cooked pasta, drained
grated Parmesan cheese (optional)

Directions

1   Heat the olive oil in the cooker and sauté the garlic for about 1 minute. Stir in the remaining sauce ingredients.

2   Lock the lid in place, bring to high pressure. Stabilize the pressure and cook for 5 minutes. Release the pressure. Serve over the cooked pasta and garnish with the grated Parmesan cheese.

Serves 4

Pressure Cooking Time
5 minutes

Wild Rice Pilaf

The nutty flavor of wild rice is showcased in this pilaf recipe that takes half the normal time to cook. This can easily be doubled or tripled for a crowd.

Ingredients

1 cup wild rice
4 cups water
1/2 teaspoon salt
1 tablespoon olive oil
1 tablespoon butter
1/2 cup minced shallot or onion
1 cup chopped bell pepper
1 cup chopped mushrooms
1 cup chopped carrots
2 tablespoons minced fresh parsley, divided
Pinch of thyme
1 cup white wine
salt and pepper if desired

Directions

1　Rinse and drain the wild rice. Place the wild rice in the pressure cooker with the 4 cups water and 1/2 teaspoon salt. Lock the lid in place, bring to high pressure. Stabilize the pressure and cook for 20 minutes. The grains will pop open. Release the pressure. Drain the wild rice, set aside and keep warm.

2　Heat the oil and butter in the pressure cooker. Stir in the onion, bell pepper, mushrooms, carrots and 1 tablespoon of minced parsley and the pinch of thyme. Sauté for a minute or two. Add the white wine and cooked wild rice.

3　Lock the lid in place, bring to high pressure. Stabilize the pressure and cook for 5 minutes. Release the pressure. Stir in the remaining tablespoon of parsley. Serve.

Serves 4-6

Pressure Cooking Time
20 minutes + 5 minutes

Mushroom Risotto

Ingredients

4 ounces shitake mushrooms
2 tablespoons light olive oil
1 1/2 cups arborio rice
3 large shallots, chopped
1 teaspoon porcini powder
1/2 cup dry white wine
2 cups (or more) low-salt chicken broth
1 teaspoon kosher salt
1 cup freshly grated Parmesan cheese (about 3 ounces)
2 tablespoons chopped fresh parsley
freshly ground pepper to taste

Directions

1. Chop mushrooms coarsely. Heat oil in your pressure cooker over medium-high heat. Add rice, shallots, and porcini powder, stir 1 minute. Add wine and cook until almost evaporated, stirring frequently, about 1 minute. Mix in 2 cups broth and salt, then mushrooms. Lock lid in place.

2. Bring to high pressure. Stabilize and cook rice 4 minutes. Release the pressure.

3. Cook rice uncovered over medium-high heat until creamy and tender but still firm to bite, stirring often and adding more broth by 1/4 cupfuls if thinner consistency is desired, about 2 minutes.

4. Mix in cheese and parsley. Season risotto to taste with pepper.

Serves 4

Pressure Cooking Time

4 minutes

Curried Squash

Ingredients

1 1/2 tablespoons vegetable oil
1 onion, chopped
2 pound butternut squash, peeled, cut in 1 inch pieces
1/2 can vegetable stock
1/4 can coconut milk
1 teaspoon red curry paste
2 tablespoons fresh cilantro, chopped

Directions

1. Heat oil in a pressure cooker over high heat. Cook onion 4-5 minutes, stirring frequently until golden. Add squash and cook 1 minute.

2. Stir in remaining ingredients, except cilantro. Secure cover and bring to high heat. Cook exactly 6 minutes. Release pressure by running cold water over lid. Add cilantro and salt to taste.

Serves 6

Pressure Cooking Time

6 minutes

beans & potatoes

Beans and potatoes have always played an important part of the Mediterranean diet, which is rich in complex carbohydrates.

One of the fastest ways to cook beans and potatoes is in a pressure cooker. What used to take hours to cook is now reduced to minutes.

Beans are also an excellent source of fiber. Some of the beans highest in fiber include navy beans, red beans, black beans, garbanzo beans (chickpeas), and kidney beans.

Potatoes have long been a favorite (& versatile) comfort food. Fortunately for potato lovers and health-conscious people, their rich complex carbohydrate content makes them a great energy food.

Boston Baked Beans

As all-American as apple pie, and so much better than canned.

Ingredients

2 cups dried, white beans
1/3 pound salt pork, diced (or slab of bacon, diced)
3 tablespoons brown sugar
2 tablespoons molasses
1/2 teaspoon mustard
1 onion diced
2 tablespoons ketchup
Water

Directions

1   Soak the beans in cold water and cover overnight. Drain.

2   Heat the cooker and sear pork on all sides. Remove
    excess drippings. Add all ingredients to the cooker
    and add enough water to cover beans well. Close lid
    and bring to pressure. Cook for 40 minutes. Release
    pressure, open lid and serve.

Serves 4

Pressure Cooking Time
40 minutes

Red Beans with Cabbage

The word is out- beans are among the most nutritious foods you can eat, and now you can make them in record time. Here is an appealing, hearty and healthy winter bean stew, beautifully complimented by sautéed cabbage. You can use the same basic recipe for white beans and chickpeas.

Ingredients

2 tablespoons olive oil
1 cup finely chopped onion
6 cloves garlic, minced
2 teaspoons paprika
1 pound dried red beans, such as red kidney beans
6 cups cold water
1 medium onion, peeled and cut in half
1 large carrot, peeled and cut in half
1 small leek, very well washed
1/4 pound piece slab bacon or salt pork, cut in 4 cubes
1/4 pound sausages- either breakfast, Italian or chorizo (optional)
Salt to taste
3 tablespoons olive oil
1/4 cup chopped onion
2 cloves garlic, minced

Cabbage:
1 small head cabbage, coarsely chopped
Salt and freshly ground pepper

Directions

1 Place the beans in water to cover and soak overnight. Drain. Heat the oil in the cooker and sauté the onion and garlic slowly until the onion is wilted. Stir in the paprika. Remove from the cooker and set aside.

2 Combine the beans in the cooker with the 6 cups water, onion halves, carrot, leek, bacon, and sausage. Close the lid, bring to pressure and cook for 15 minutes. Release pressure and remove the lid. Add the reserved sautéed onion and garlic, salt to taste, close the lid and bring to pressure again. Complete cooking for an additional 20 minutes.

3 While the beans finish cooking, prepare the cabbage in a skillet. Heat the oil, add the onion and garlic and sauté until the onion is wilted. Add the cabbage, salt and pepper to taste and stir-fry about 10 minutes. Cover and continue cooking to taste.

4 Release the pressure and remove the lid. Serve the beans in soup bowls with a generous dollop of the cabbage in each bowl and accompanied by crusty bread.

Serves 4

Pressure Cooking Time
15 minutes + 20 minutes

Orange-Flavored Candied Yams

Ingredients

1 cup orange juice
2 large sweet potatoes
1/2 teaspoon salt
1/2 cup brown sugar
1 teaspoon grated orange zest
2 tablespoons butter

Directions

1   Pour the orange juice into the cooker. Peel the yams
and cut them in half lengthwise. Arrange in the
cooker and sprinkle with salt, brown sugar and
orange zest. Dot with butter.

2   Close the lid and bring to high pressure, then lower
heat and cook for 7 minutes.

3   Release pressure and remove lid.

4   Lift out the yams. Boil down the sauce until thickened
and pour over the yams. Serve.

Serves 2-3

Pressure Cooking Time

7 minutes

Herbed Garlic Mashed Potatoes

Ingredients

3 large potatoes, peeled and cubed
1 cup chicken broth
1 cup warm skim milk
2 tablespoons olive oil
1 tablespoon minced thyme
1/2 teaspoon garlic powder
1/2 teaspoon dried rosemary, crushed
1/2 teaspoon salt
1/4 teaspoon pepper
3 cloves of garlic, minced

Directions

1 In pressure cooker, add potatoes, minced garlic and broth. Close lid, bring to high pressure, stabilize and cook for 6 minutes.

2 Release pressure. Open lid and drain broth, leaving only 1/4 cup of broth remaining.

3 Add the warm milk and olive oil. Beat with mixer until potatoes are fluffy.

4 Add the herbs, salt and pepper. Serve while hot.

Makes 4-6 servings

Pressure Cooking Time
6 minutes

German Potato Salad

Ingredients

3 pounds large boiling potatoes (about 6)
1 teaspoon celery seeds
3/4 cup water
1 tablespoon Dijon-style mustard
1/2 pound of lean bacon (about 8 slices),
    cut crosswise into 1/2-inch pieces
6 tablespoons cider vinegar
1/2 cup water
1 cup finely chopped onion
3 hard-boiled large eggs, chopped
1 cup thinly sliced celery
1/3 cup chopped dill pickles
1 tablespoon sugar
1/2 cup thinly sliced scallion greens
2 tablespoons all-purpose flour
Salt and pepper to taste

Directions

1 Quarter the potatoes lengthwise and cut them crosswise into 1/2-inch pieces. In steamer basket, add potatoes and place in pressure cooker with water.

2 Close lid, bring to high pressure, then lower heat and pressure cook for 5 minutes. Release pressure, open lid, drain water and remove potatoes to bowl.

3 Hardboil 3 eggs. Once cooked, chop into pieces.

4 In a large heavy skillet, cook bacon over moderate heat, stirring, until it is crisp, then transfer to paper towels to drain.

5 Pour off all but 4 tablespoons of the fat, and add to skillet onion and celery – cook the mixture over moderately low heat, stirring, until onion is softened. Add the sugar, flour and celery seeds, and cook for 30 seconds, stirring often. Stir in the mustard, vinegar, and 1/2 cup of water, bring mixture to a boil, stirring, then lower heat and simmer for 2 minutes, or until mixture is thickened. Season the dressing with salt and pepper, pour it over the potatoes, and stir in the eggs, pickles, bacon and scallion greens.

6 Serve the salad warm.

Serves 8

Pressure Cooking Time
5 minutes

Apple Potato Salad

Ingredients

4 small new potatoes
1 Golden Delicious Apple
4 celery stalks
1/4 cup Creamy Dill dressing
1/4 teaspoon dill
Lemon juice

Directions

1. Slice the potatoes into bite-sized pieces. Place in pressure cooker with 1/2 cup water. Close lid, bring to high pressure, and cook for 4 minutes. Release pressure using cold water release method. Drain and place in a pan of ice water.

2. Peel the apple and slice into bite-sized pieces (sprinkle with lemon juice so it won't brown).

3. Finely chop the celery.

4. Combine all ingredients and mix with dressing and dill. Chill several hours.

Serves 4

Pressure Cooking Time
4 minutes

Garlic Rosemary Potatoes

The perfect accompaniment to grilled steaks or fish.

Ingredients

1 1/2 pounds small red new potatoes
3 cloves garlic, minced
1 tablespoon fresh rosemary, more if desired
3 tablespoons olive oil
1/2 teaspoon salt
1/2 teaspoon pepper

Directions

1 Scrub the potatoes and leave whole. In a bowl, toss the potatoes with the remaining ingredients to coat them well.

2 Place a steamer basket on a trivet in the pressure cooker and add water to just under the basket. Place the seasoned potatoes in the basket.

3 Lock the lid in place, bring to high pressure. Stabilize the pressure and cook for 7 minutes. Release the pressure.

4 Transfer to a bowl. If too much of the seasoning has steamed off, add a bit more oil and rosemary and toss before serving.

Serves 4

Pressure Cooking Time
7 minutes

Bean and Pepper Salad

Ingredients

3/4 cup dried black beans
3/4 cup dried red or kidney beans
1 yellow bell pepper
1 red bell pepper
1 fresh poblano chili pepper
1/4 cup red wine vinegar
1 teaspoon salt
1/2 teaspoon freshly ground black pepper
1 canned chipotle chili pepper in vinegar or in adobo
    sauce, stemmed, seeded, and minced (optional)
2/3 cup olive oil
1 red onion, finely diced

Directions

1 Sort through beans and discard any stones or other foreign matter. Rinse well and place in large bowl of boiling water for one hour, which helps speed up the cooking process.

2 After soaking, place beans in pressure cooker, bring to high pressure, then stabilize and cook for 18 minutes. Release pressure using automatic or cold-water release method.

3 Open lid and drain beans in a colander and spread them on plate to cool slightly.

4 Remove the stems, seeds and ribs from the bell peppers and poblano chili. Cut the peppers into 1/4-inch dice, or a size as small as the cooked beans.

5 In a large bowl, whisk together the vinegar, salt, black pepper and chipotle chili. Slowly add the olive oil, whisking constantly. Toss in the diced peppers, onion and warm beans and mix well.

6 Cover and refrigerate for at least two hours or as long as overnight. Serve the salad chilled.

Serves 4

Pressure Cooking Time
18 minutes

Cold Pinto Bean Salad

Serve with Pulled pork and warmed tortillas for an easy dinner.

Ingredients

1/2 pound pinto beans
1 tablespoon olive oil
2 medium avocados, diced
2 tomatoes, diced
1 yellow bell pepper diced
3 green onions, sliced
1/4 cup packed cilantro, minced

Dressing:
2/3 cup sour cream
1 tablespoon chili powder
1 tablespoon ground cumin
1/2 teaspoon oregano
salt and pepper to taste

Garnish:
iceberg lettuce

Directions

1 Quick soak the beans by placing them in the pressure cooker with 4 cups water. Lock the lid in place, bring to high pressure. Stabilize the pressure and cook for 2 minutes. Release the pressure. Drain and rinse the beans in cold water.

2 Return the beans to the pressure cooker along with the oil (to reduce foaming), season with salt and cover with 4 cups water. Lock the lid in place, bring to high pressure. Stabilize the pressure and cook for 7 minutes. Release the pressure. Drain and rinse the beans.

3 Combine the beans with the avocado, bell pepper, tomato, cilantro and scallions. Combine the dressing ingredients together in a small bowl and pour over the bean salad. Use the lettuce leaves to serve as cups for the salad.

Serves 4-6

Pressure Cooking Time
2 minutes + 7 minutes

Edamame Salad

Edamame, or soy beans, are available both fresh or frozen, and with or without their exterior pods.

Ingredients

1 lb shelled edamame beans, fresh or frozen
1/4 cup minced red onion
1 can (11 ounces) mandarin oranges
1/4 cup minced cilantro
salt and pepper
1/2 cup cashews
1/2 cup mayonnaise, nonfat can be used
1 large ripe mango, diced

Serves 4

Pressure Cooking Time
5 minutes

Directions

1   Place a steamer basket on a trivet in the pressure cooker, and add water to just under the basket, place the edamame and red onion in the basket.

2   Lock the lid in place, bring to high pressure. Stabilize the pressure and cook for 5 minutes. Release the pressure. Drain the edamame and onions and set aside. Drain the mandarin oranges and reserve the juice.

3   In a large bowl, whisk the reserved juice from the mandarin oranges into the mayonnaise. Season with salt and pepper. Stir in the cilantro. Add the edamame, mandarin oranges, mango and cashews. Gently toss. Chill until ready to serve.

Mexican Black Bean Chili

Ingredients

1 1/2 cup dried black beans, rinsed
4 cups water
2 pounds butternut squash, washed, peeled, seeded, and cut into 8 pieces
1/4 cup sour cream or plain yogurt
1 large yam, peeled, & cut into 6 pieces
4 garlic cloves, peeled and minced
2-3 canned chipotle peppers
1 tablespoon olive oil

Condiments:
1 red pepper (diced)
1 large tomato (diced)
1 ripe avocado (peeled, pitted & sliced)
1 small onion (diced)
6 tablespoons chopped cilantro
2 limes, cut into wedges

Directions

1   Rinse the black beans in colander under cold water. Place in large bowl, cover with 4 cups of water and allow to soak 6-8 hours, or overnight. Reserve liquid. (This can be ommited if using canned beans.)

2   Heat olive oil in pressure cooker on medium-high heat. Add garlic and chipotles and sauté 30 seconds. Add squash, yam and beans, along with soaking liquid. Stir well.

3   Close lid, bring to high pressure, then lower heat on stove and cook for 15 minutes.

4   Release pressure using cold-water release method.

5   Discard chipotles.

6   Mash the beans, yam and squash by pressing them against the side of the pot with the back of a spoon.

7   Serve in large soup bowls and allow guests to add condiments.

Serves 6-8

Pressure Cooking Time
15 minutes

Basic Lentils

Lentils need a bit of seasoning to brighten their earthy flavor.

Ingredients

1 tablespoon olive oil
1 cup lentils, picked over
2 cups stock or water
1 cup bell pepper, diced
2 cloves garlic, minced
1/2 teaspoon dried thyme

Directions

1   In the pressure cooker, heat the oil over moderate heat and add the garlic. Sauté until transparent. Add the remaining ingredients and stir well. If using water instead of stock - add 1/2 teaspoon of salt.

2   Lock the lid in place, bring to high pressure. Stabilize the pressure and cook for 12 minutes. Release the pressure and serve.

Serves 4

Pressure Cooking Time
12 minutes

Mashed Gingered
Sweet Potatoes

Ingredients

- 2 1/2 pounds sweet potatoes
- 1 tablespoon minced, fresh ginger root
- 3/4 cup chicken stock (or water)
- 2 tablespoons butter
- 1/2 cup milk (or cream)
- salt & pepper- optional

Directions

1. Peel and cube the sweet potatoes. Place in cooker with ginger and stock. Lock lid into place and bring to high pressure. Stabilize the heat and cook for 10 minutes. Release pressure. Drain any excess water from the potatoes.

2. Stir in milk and butter and mash the mixture until smooth. Season with salt and pepper.

Serves 4

Pressure Cooking Time
10 minutes

Hummus Dip

Ingredients

- 1 cup dried garbanzo (chick peas, cici) beans
- 3 cloves garlic
- 1/4 cup tahini, (sesame seed paste)
- 1/4 cup olive oil
- 1/4 cup fresh squeezed lemon juice
- 1 teaspoon salt

Serves 6

Pressure Cooking Time

18 minutes

Directions

1. Rinse beans and remove any debris. In a large bowl, soak beans in water to cover for 4-6 hours. Drain. Place beans with 3 cups water in pressure cooker and a bit of oil to reduce foaming.

2. Close lid and bring to high pressure. Stabilize heat and cook for 18 minutes at high pressure. Release pressure and allow beans to cool in the cooking liquid. Rinse and drain beans.

3. In a food processor or blender, puree the cooked beans and garlic. Add tahini, lemon juice and salt. With machine running, drizzle in the olive oil. If too thick, drizzle in a bit of water while the machine is running. Add more salt if desired. Serve with toasted pita bread or vegetables.

Lentil Casserole

Almost a meal in itself. Double the stock and it becomes a hearty soup.

Ingredients

1 tablespoon olive oil
1 1/2 cups lentils, picked over
3 1/2 cups chicken or beef stock
1 cup carrots, diced
1 cup red bell pepper, diced
1 cup celery, diced
2 cloves garlic, minced
1 cup onion, diced
1/4 cup sun dried tomatoes, diced
1 tablespoon dried thyme
1 teaspoon dried basil

Directions

1   In the pressure cooker, heat the oil over medium heat and add the onions and garlic. Sauté until transparent. Add the remaining ingredients and stir well.

2   Lock the lid in place, bring to high pressure. Stabilize the pressure and cook for 20 minutes. Release the pressure and serve.

Serves 4

Pressure Cooking Time
20 minutes

Pesto Potatoes

Leave the potatoes in chunks for a rustic presentation or mash and serve with a dollop of butter in the middle.

Ingredients

2 pounds russet potatoes, peeled and cut
into large chunks
1/2 teaspoon salt
1/2 teaspoon pepper
1/4 cup prepared pesto
2 tablespoons grated parmesan cheese

Directions

1　Place a steamer basket on trivet in the pressure cooker and add water to just under the basket. Place the potatoes in the basket and sprinkle with the salt.

2　Lock the lid in place, bring to high pressure. Stabilize the pressure and cook for 5 minutes. Release the pressure. Transfer to a bowl. Toss gently with the remaining ingredients and serve.

Serves 4

Pressure Cooking Time

5 minutes

Picnic Beans

A bit sweet and a bit spicy, these beans are wonderful with barbecued hamburgers.

Ingredients

8 ounces small red beans, cleaned and rinsed
1/4 lb diced bacon
1/2 cup diced bell pepper
1/2 cup diced yellow onion
2 tablespoons bourbon
1/2 cup molasses
1 tablespoon prepared mustard
2 tablespoons balsamic vinegar
1 14.5 ounce can diced tomatoes, no salt
2/3 cup water
1 teaspoon salt

Directions

1 Quick soak the beans by placing the rinsed and cleaned beans in the pressure cooker with 3 cups water. Lock lid into place and bring to high pressure. Stabilize the heat and cook for 2 minutes. Release pressure. Rinse and drain the beans and set aside.

2 In the pressure cooker, brown the diced bacon over medium heat. Once cooked, drain the bacon and set aside until later. Leave 2 tablespoons of bacon fat in the pressure cooker, discard the rest. In the reserved bacon fat, sauté the bell peppers and onions until translucent. Stir in the beans, molasses, bourbon, prepared mustard, water and balsamic vinegar.

3 Lock lid into place and bring to high pressure. Stabilize the heat and cook for 25 minutes. Release pressure and stir in salt and reserved bacon pieces. Season to taste and serve.

Serves 4

Pressure Cooking Time

2 minutes + 25 minutes

Pinto Beans with Chilies and Cheese

Better than any can of store bought beans. Wonderful as a side dish or inside a tortilla.

Ingredients

1 lb pinto beans, rinsed and picked over
2 tablespoons olive oil
1 large onion, chopped
2 garlic cloves, minced
6-8 ounces of chorizo sausage, diced
2 large chilies, seeded and diced
3 cups chicken stock
2 teaspoons chili powder
1 tablespoon ground cumin
1/2 teaspoon salt
1 1/2 cups grated sharp cheddar cheese

Directions

1 In the pressure cooker, place the pinto beans and 3 cups of water. Lock the lid in place, bring to high pressure. Stabilize the pressure and cook for 2 minutes. Release the pressure. Drain and rinse the beans under cold running water.

2 Heat 1 tablespoon of the olive in the bottom of the cooker. Add the onion, chorizo, garlic and chilies. Cook about 2 minutes. Add the beans to the vegetables in the cooker with 3 cups chicken stock, chili powder, cumin and remaining 1 tablespoon of oil.

3 Lock the lid in place, bring to high pressure. Stabilize the pressure and cook for 8 minutes. Release the pressure. Drain the beans, reserve the liquid and return the beans to the pot. Stir in the salt. If desired, mash a portion of the beans with the addition of the reserved cooking liquid. Over very low heat, stir in the cheese until melted.

Serves 6-8

Pressure Cooking Time
2 minutes + 8 minutes

Potato Artichoke Salad

Ingredients

12 ounces frozen artichoke hearts, thawed
2 tablespoons olive oil
2 cloves of garlic
salt and fresh ground pepper to taste
1/4 cup water
2 lbs new potatoes, quartered
1/4 cup minced fresh parsley
1 tablespoon fresh rosemary
1/2 cup olive oil
1/4 cup balsamic vinegar
1 cup cherry tomatoes, halved
1 cup celery, diced

Directions

1. In the pressure cooker, heat the olive oil over medium high heat and stir in the garlic. Add the artichokes, season with salt and pepper, and sauté about 4 minutes. Add 1/4 cup of water. Lock the lid in place, bring to high pressure. Stabilize the pressure and cook for 2 minutes. Release the pressure.

2. Remove the artichokes and set aside. Place a steamer basket on a trivet in the pressure cooker, and add water to just under the basket, add the potatoes to the basket. Season with salt and pepper.

3. Lock the lid in place, bring to high pressure. Stabilize the pressure and cook for 5 minutes. Release the pressure. Remove the potatoes to the bowl of artichokes and stir in the parsley, fresh rosemary, 1/2 cup olive oil, and balsamic vinegar. Add the celery and cherry tomatoes. Mix well. Serve warm or cold.

Serves 4-6

Pressure Cooking Time
2 minutes + 5 minutes

Three Bean Salad
with Creamy Dressing

This traditional salad has brighter flavors when made fresh and worth the extra time needed to cook each bean separately.

Ingredients

3/4 lb fresh green beans
1 cup garbanzo beans, rinsed and sorted
1 cup kidney beans, rinsed and sorted
salt and oil as needed
6 cups chicken stock, divided

Dressing:
1 cup non-fat mayonnaise
2 tablespoons olive oil
1/4 cup balsamic vinegar
1 teaspoon sugar
1/2 teaspoon salt
1/4 teaspoon pepper
1/4 teaspoon dried oregano
1/4 teaspoon dried basil
juice of 1/2 lemon

Directions

1 Pressure cook the green beans on high for 2 minutes. Release pressure. Drain the green beans and rinse under cold water to stop the cooking. Place in a large bowl and refrigerate.

2 In the pressure cooker, place the garbanzo beans in 3 cups water. Lock the lid in place, bring to high pressure. Stabilize the pressure and cook for 2 minutes. Release the pressure. Drain and rinse the beans under cold running water. Return the beans to the cooker with 3 cups chicken stock and 1 tablespoon of oil.

3 Lock the lid in place, bring to high pressure. Stabilize the pressure and cook for 25 minutes. Release the pressure. Drain and rinse the beans under cold running water and add to the cooked green beans. In the pressure cooker, place the kidney beans with 3 cups water.

4 Lock the lid in place, bring to high pressure. Stabilize the pressure and cook for 2 minutes. Release the pressure. Drain and rinse the beans under cold running water. Return the beans to the cooker with 3 cups chicken stock and 1 tablespoon of oil.

5 Lock the lid in place, bring to high pressure. Stabilize the pressure and cook for 10 minutes. Release the pressure. Drain and rinse the beans under cold running water and add them to the cooked green beans. Whisk together the dressing ingredients and pour over the prepared beans. Refrigerate until ready to serve.

Serves 4

Pressure Cooking Time
41 minutes (total)

Seasoned Black Beans

This is a terrific side dish to pulled pork.

Ingredients

1/2 pound black beans
1 tablespoon olive oil
1/4 lb bacon, diced
1 onion, diced
1 clove garlic, minced
2 ancho chilies, diced

Directions

1　Quick soak the beans by placing them in the pressure cooker with 4 cups water. Lock the lid in place, bring to high pressure. Stabilize the pressure and cook for 2 minutes. Release the pressure. Drain and rinse the beans in cold water.

2　Return the beans to the pressure cooker along with the 1 tablespoon oil (to reduce foaming), season with salt and cover with 4 cups water. Lock the lid in place, bring to high pressure. Stabilize the pressure and cook for 7 minutes. Release the pressure. Drain, rinse the beans and set aside.

3　In the pressure cooker, sauté the diced bacon over medium heat. Remove the cooked bacon with a slotted spoon and set aside. Remove all but 2 tablespoons of the bacon fat and use this to sauté the onion, garlic and chilies.

4　When the onion is transparent, return the beans and reserved bacon to the cooker. Season with salt and pepper. Simmer for 5 minutes to allow the seasonings to blend.

Serves 4

Pressure Cooking Time

2 minutes + 7 minutes

White Beans
with Sausage and Peppers

A hearty version of traditional sausage and peppers.

Ingredients

1/2 lb small white beans
1 tablespoon olive oil
1 teaspoon salt
2 tablespoons olive oil
1 clove garlic, minced
3 Italian sausages, sliced
2 bell peppers, sliced
1 medium onion, sliced
pinch anise seed (optional)
1 14 ounce can diced tomatoes
1 teaspoon died oregano

Directions

1   Quick soak the beans by placing them in the pressure cooker with 4 cups water. Lock the lid in place, bring to high pressure. Stabilize the pressure and cook for 2 minutes. Release the pressure. Drain and rinse the beans in cold water.

2   Return the beans to the pressure cooker along with the 1 tablespoon oil (to reduce foaming), season with salt and cover with 4 cups water. Lock the lid in place, bring to high pressure. Stabilize the pressure and cook for 4 minutes. Release the pressure. Drain and rinse the beans. Set aside.

3   In the pressure cooker heat the 2 tablespoons olive oil over medium heat and sauté the onion, bell peppers, garlic, sausage and anise seeds until everything is cooked through. Add the beans, tomatoes, and dried oregano. Simmer for 5 minutes to allow the seasonings to blend.

Serves 4-6

Pressure Cooking Time
2 minutes + 4 minutes

Orange Laced Sweet Potatoes

Ingredients

1 cup orange juice
Grated zest of 1 orange
1/2 teaspoon ground cinnamon
1/8 teaspoon grated nutmeg
5 large sweet potatoes (3 pounds),
  peeled and cut into 1/4 inch slices
1/3 cup orange marmalade
2-3 tablespoons sweet butter, cut into bits
Salt to taste
1/3 cup coarsely chopped walnuts (optional)

Serves 8

Pressure Cooking Time
5 minutes

Directions

1 Combine the orange juice, zest, cinnamon and
   nutmeg in the cooker.

2 Place the sweet potato slices in the liquid and top
   with marmalade and butter. Lock the lid in place and
   bring to high pressure. Stabilize and cook for 5
   minutes. Reduce pressure using the quick-release
   method. Remove the lid.

3 Adjust the seasoning, adding salt to taste as you stir in
   the walnuts and create a coarse mash. Transfer to a
   heated serving bowl and serve immediately.

Indian Style Lentils

Traditionally this Indian dish is baked in the tandoor oven, but you get a similar result in the pressure cooker in 30 minutes.

Ingredients

1 1/2 cups whole black (or other) lentils (urad dal)
5 cups water
2 teaspoons cumin seeds
2 teaspoons coriander seeds
1 medium yellow onion (about 8 ounces),
   quartered and finely sliced
1 large ripe tomato (about 8 ounces),
   cored and coarsely chopped
1 generous tablespoon tomato paste
2 fresh green chiles (serrano or jalapeno),
   minced(seeded if desired)
4 large garlic cloves,
   smashed and coarsely chopped
1 tablespoon peeled and grated ginger root
1 teaspoon cayenne powder
1/2 cinnamon stick
4 tablespoons butter
1 teaspoon salt (or to taste)
1/4 cup heavy cream (or half-and-half)
Juice of half a lemon
Chopped fresh coriander
   (cilantro) leaves (about 2 tablespoons)

Directions

1 Spread the lentils on a large tray and carefully pick over, discarding any tiny stones or bits of grit. Place in a colander and swish under running water with your fingers and rinse several times. Place lentils in pressure cooker and add water.

2 Toast the cumin and coriander seeds together in a small pan and grind with a mortar and pestle or in a coffee grinder. Add to lentils. Stir in the onion, tomato, tomato paste, chiles, garlic, ginger, cayenne, cinnamon stick and butter.

3 Cook for 30 minutes at high pressure. Allow pressure to drop naturally. Open lid and add salt and cream. Stir well and add lemon juice. Garnish with cilantro.

Serves 8

Pressure Cooking Time
30 minutes

meats

MEATS

When cooking red meats in a pressure cooker, there's no need to use expensive cuts of beef. Lesser quality cuts of meat work just as well as they become tender and full of flavor in a pressure cooker.

POULTRY

There are so many varieties of meals you can make with poultry, its no wonder chicken is such a popular meat in the United States. Chicken and turkey can be pressure cooked in as little as 6 minutes, and when combined with vegetables, rice or potatoes, you can have a meal in less than 15 minutes – and made all in one pot.

Sweet and Sour Spare Ribs

As good or better than any you are likely to find in a Chinese restaurant.

Ingredients

3 tablespoons oil

3 pounds lean spare ribs, each rib cut in 3 pieces

Sweet Sour Sauce:

3 tablespoons soy sauce

2 tablespoons brown sugar

3 tablespoons honey

3 cloves garlic, minced

1 /4 cup ketchup

2 tablespoons minced onion

2 tablespoons apricot marmalade

2 tablespoons cider vinegar

2 tablespoons dry sherry

1 teaspoon hot pepper sauce, or to taste

Serves 4

Pressure Cooking Time

15 minutes

Directions

1 In a small bowl combine all the sauce ingredients.

2 Heat the oil in the cooker until very hot, then add as many ribs at a time as will comfortably fit, and brown well. Pour off all fat, then stir in the sauce. Close the lid and bring to high pressure. Stabilize and cook for 15 minutes.

Herb Roasted Chicken

Quick cooking and a minimal amount of liquid produces this juicy, tender and flavorful chicken dish. If possible, use fresh herbs for a more assertive fragrance.

Ingredients

3 pounds chicken cut into pieces
3 medium tomatoes, sliced
1/4 cup chicken broth or stock
1/4 cup parsley, chopped
1 tablespoon fresh rosemary
1 tablespoon fresh sage, chopped
Hot, cooked brown or white rice
Salt and pepper to taste

Directions

1
Heat butter in the pressure cooker and brown chicken on all sides. Remove chicken and sauté onions until golden brown. Add tomatoes, parsley, chicken stock, salt and pepper. Add chicken and herbs.

2
Close lid and bring to high pressure. Stabilize pressure and cook for 15 minutes. Release pressure, remove lid and serve over the white or brown rice.

Serves 4

Pressure Cooking Time

15 minutes

Braised Veal with Carrots

Ingredients

4 tablespoons olive oil
2 large onions, chopped
1 clove garlic, minced
1 tablespoon fresh rosemary, chopped
2 pounds cubed veal for stew
1 cup Marsala or other sweet wine
1 pound carrots, peeled and grated
1 1/2 cups beef broth
Freshly ground pepper to taste

Serves 4-6

Pressure Cooking Time
10 minutes

Directions

1   Warm 2 tablespoons of olive oil in pressure cooker pot over low heat. Add the onions, garlic and rosemary and sauté until tender and translucent, about 8 minutes. Remove from cooker and set aside in bowl.

2   In cooker, warm the remaining 2 tablespoons of olive oil over high heat. Add the meat and brown well on all sides, sprinkling a little salt after it has browned. Add the wine and let it bubble up. Add the sautéed onions, the carrots, and the broth to cover.

3   Close lid, bring to high pressure, stabilize and cook for 10 minutes.

4   Release pressure, open lid and season with salt and pepper before serving.

Pork Chops

Ingredients

2 tablespoons canola oil
4 lean pork chops with bone
2 large potatoes, sliced
2-3 carrots, sliced
1 medium onion, thinly sliced or chopped
2 cans cream of mushroom soup with roasted garlic
1/2 cup white wine
Salt and pepper to taste

Serves 4

Pressure Cooking Time

10 minutes

Directions

1   In pressure cooker pot, add oil and brown pork chops. Remove and set aside.

2   Place sliced potatoes, carrots and onions in pressure cooker.

3   Top potatoes with browned chops.

4   Combine the 2 cans of mushroom soup, wine and season with salt and pepper and pour over pork chops.

5   Close lid, bring to high pressure, stabilize and cook for 10 minutes. Let pressure cool down naturally. Open lid and serve.

Meatballs

Serve with your favorite pasta.

Ingredients

2 pounds lean ground meat
1 cup flavored bread crumbs
1 onion, minced
2 tablespoons Romano cheese, grated
1 egg
1/4 cup milk
2 tablespoons tomato paste
2 tablespoons olive oil
1 cup beef broth
2 small cans of tomato sauce
1 teaspoon oregano
1/2 teaspoon salt
1/8 teaspoon pepper

Serves 8

Pressure Cooking Time

4 minutes

Directions

1   In a large bowl, mix meat, bread crumbs, tomato paste, onion, cheese, egg and milk. Mix well. Form into small balls.

2   In pressure cooker, add olive oil and brown meatballs. After browning, add broth and tomato sauce, oregano, salt and pepper.

3   Close lid on cooker, bring to pressure, stabilize and cook for 4 minutes.

4   Use cold-water release method to release pressure. Open lid and serve.

Sirloin Strips
with Carmelized Onions

Ingredients

3 tablespoons olive oil

2 large onions, cut in half and sliced thin

1 large red bell pepper, seeded, cored, cut in half
and sliced into thin strips

2 teaspoons dried basil

1 tablespoon brown sugar

1 tablespoon balsamic vinegar

2 strips lean bacon, chopped into small pieces

2 pounds lean sirloin steak, cut into fillets and
sliced into 1/2-inch strips

2 tablespoons cornstarch

3/4 cup hearty ale or dark beer

1/2 teaspoon ground allspice or

2 whole allspice berries

1 bay leaf

1 tablespoon honey mustard

Directions

1   Heat 2 tablespoons olive oil in pressure cooker over
medium high heat.

2   Add onion, red pepper, dried basil and sauté 5
minutes, stirring frequently. Add sugar and
balsamic vinegar.

3   Reduce heat to low and continue cooking until soft
and golden, about 5-8 minutes. Stir frequently so that
onions do not brown. Remove from pressure cooker
to a bowl and set aside.

4   Raise heat to medium high, add the bacon to
pressure cooker and cook until just browned. Remove
bacon to a small bowl with a slotted spoon.

5   Add the remaining tablespoon of olive oil to the
bacon drippings. Raise heat to high. Brown the beef
in two batches until browned on all sides. Return
browned meat and any collected juices to the
pressure cooker. Sprinkle with the cornstarch and
cook 1 minute. Add the browned bacon, beer,
allspice, and bay leaf. Stir well.

6   Position lid on cooker and lock in place. Bring to high
pressure, stabilize and cook for 12 minutes. Remove
from heat and release pressure using cold-water
release method.

7   Open cooker, add the sautéed onion and red pepper
and the honey mustard. Replace the lid, bring up to
high pressure and cook additional 5 minutes.

8   Remove from heat and release pressure using cold-water
release method. Season with salt and pepper to taste.

9   Remove and discard the bay leaf before serving.

Serves 6-8

Pressure Cooking Time

12 minutes + 5 minutes

Asian Chicken

Authentic Asian flavors without having to call for take out.

Ingredients

1/2 cup slivered almonds
1 tablespoon olive oil
1 tablespoon toasted sesame oil
4 cloves garlic, minced
1 tablespoon minced fresh ginger
1 pound boneless skinless chicken breasts
1/2 medium onion
2 large carrots, diced
2 celery ribs, diced
1/4 cup hoisin sauce blended with 2 tablespoons water
1 tablespoon soy sauce
cooked rice

Serves 4

Pressure Cooking Time

8 minutes

Directions

1 In the pressure cooker over medium heat, toast the slivered almonds. Remove the almonds and set aside.

2 Heat the olive and sesame oils in the pressure cooker, stir in garlic and ginger. Add the chicken and lightly brown on all sides. Stir in the remaining ingredients except the rice.

3 Lock the lid in place, bring to high pressure. Stabilize the pressure and cook for 8 minutes. Release the pressure. Serve the chicken over the cooked rice. Pour pan sauce over the top and garnish with the toasted almonds.

Spanish Gold Sautéed Chicken

Ingredients

- 1 tablespoon olive oil
- 1/2 teaspoon each: salt, lemon pepper seasoning, ground cumin
- 4 boneless chicken breast halves
- 1 medium leek, white part only, chopped
- 2 garlic cloves, minced
- 3 lemon slices, 1/4-inch thick
- 1/2 cup pitted prunes
- 1/3 cup pitted green olives, cut in half
- 2 tablespoons minced fresh or 2 teaspoons dried thyme
- 1 cup orange juice
- 1/2 cup Rioja or other dry red wine
- 1/2 cup low sodium chicken broth
- 2 tablespoons honey
- 1 large plum tomato, seeded, diced
- 3 cups hot cooked rice

Directions

1 In pressure cooker, warm olive oil over high heat. Combine salt, lemon pepper seasoning and cumin; sprinkle over both sides of chicken breasts.

2 Add chicken to pressure cooker and sauté on both sides, about 5 minutes. Transfer chicken to plate and keep warm.

3 Reduce heat to medium-high. Add leek and garlic, cook and stir about 3 minutes. Add chicken, lemon slices, prunes, olives and thyme.

4 Combine orange juice, wine, chicken broth and honey; pour over chicken.

5 Close lid, bring to high pressure, stabilize and cook for 25 minutes.

6 Remove from heat and release using cold-water release method. Remove lid, set cooker back on stove and stir in tomatoes. Turn heat to low and cook for approximately 2 minutes, stirring frequently.

7 Serve chicken mixture over rice. Sprinkle with parsley. Garnish with lemon slices.

Serves 4

Pressure Cooking Time
25 minutes

Sauerkraut & Apple Pork Chops

Ingredients

- 2 tablespoons vegetable oil
- 4 pork loin chops (1-1/4 to 1-1/2 pounds total), 3/4 inch thick
- 1/2 teaspoon salt
- 1/4 teaspoon black pepper
- 3 medium-sized sweet potatoes (about 1-1/2 pounds), peeled and cut into 2-inch chunks
- 3 Red Delicious apples, peeled, cored, and cut in half
- 1/2 cup apple juice
- 1/2 cup packed light brown sugar
- 2 teaspoons ground cinnamon
- 2 pounds sauerkraut, rinsed, drained, and squeezed dry

Directions

1 Heat the oil in pressure cooker over high heat. Season the pork chops with the salt and pepper. Add 2 chops to the pressure cooker and brown uncovered for 2 to 3 minutes per side. Remove to a platter and brown the remaining 2 chops.

2 Place the sweet potatoes in the bottom of the pressure cooker then layer the pork chops and apples over them.

3 In a small bowl, combine the apple juice, brown sugar, and cinnamon; mix well and pour over the pork chops. Top with the sauerkraut, making sure not to fill the cooker more than two-thirds full.

4 Lock the lid in place and bring to high pressure. Stabilize and cook for 10 minutes.

5 Release pressure. Remove the lid and serve the pork chops with the sweet potatoes, apples, and sauerkraut, spooning the liquid in the cooker over everything.

Serves 4

Pressure Cooking Time

10 minutes

Acapulco Chicken

Ingredients

2 thick whole boneless chicken breasts
1/4 cup olive oil
3 tablespoons brown sugar
1 teaspoon cinnamon
1/2 teaspoon grated ginger
1 1/2 cups orange juice
1 cup rice
1/2 cup raisins
1/2 cup orange marmalade
1/2 cup flaked coconut
Salt and Pepper to taste

Directions

1 In saucepan, heat orange juice, raisins and marmalade until marmalade melts. Remove from heat and set aside.

2 Cut up chicken into 1 inch chunks.

3 Heat olive oil in pressure cooker and add chicken chunks. Lightly brown. Add the orange juice mixture plus the brown sugar, cinnamon, ginger and rice.

4 Close lid, bring to high pressure. Stabilize and cook for 10 minutes.

5 Remove from heat and release pressure using cold-water release method. Open, stir, and add salt and pepper to taste. To serve, place chicken and rice on dish and sprinkle with flaked coconut.

Serves 4

Pressure Cooking Time
10 minutes

Lamb Shanks Osso Buco

Ingredients

4 lamb shanks, about 1 pound each
1/2 cup flour
1 tablespoon olive oil
2 slices smoked bacon, diced
2 yellow onions, chopped
1 fennel bulb, chopped
1 red bell pepper, seeded and chopped
2 medium carrots, peeled and chopped
1/2 cup celery, chopped
4 cloves garlic, minced
28 ounces canned tomatoes, diced, undrained
3 tablespoons fresh parsley, chopped
1 teaspoon dried rosemary, crushed
1 teaspoon dried thyme
2 bay leaves
1 teaspoon grated orange zest
1/4 teaspoon ground nutmeg
1 tablespoon tomato paste
1/2 teaspoon fresh ground black pepper
1 teaspoon sugar
1 cup beef stock
1/2 cup red dry wine

Directions

1   Cut lamb shanks in half. Place flour in brown paper sack or large plastic bag; add lamb shanks and shake until coated with flour. Shake off any excess flour.

2   Heat olive oil in pressure cooker over medium heat. Add bacon and cook for 30 seconds. Add the lamb shanks and brown on both sides (you may have to do this in 2 batches). Remove the shanks and set aside.

3   Add onions, fennel, red bell pepper, carrots, celery, and garlic and cook until all vegetables are soft, about 5 minutes. Add remaining ingredients to the pot and stir; place shanks on top of the mixture.

4   Place lid on cooker, close and bring up to high pressure, stabilize and cook for 35 minutes. Release pressure and serve.

5   Garnish with fennel fronds, if desired.

Serves 8

Pressure Cooking Time
35 minutes

Brisket

Texas–style brisket in under an hour.

Ingredients

3 pounds beef brisket
Texas style dry barbecue rub
1/4 cup molasses
1/4 cup balsamic vinegar
1/4 cup water
1/4 cup barbecue sauce
1 tablespoon Worcestershire™ sauce
1 tablespoon Tabasco™ sauce

Serves 4

Pressure Cooking Time
25 minutes + 20 minutes

Directions

1 Generously season the brisket on both sides with the dry rub. In the pressure cooker, combine the molasses, vinegar, Worcestershire™ sauce, barbecue sauce, water and Tabasco™. Add the seasoned brisket.

2 Lock the lid in place, bring to high pressure. Stabilize the pressure and cook for 25 minutes. Release the pressure and turn the meat over.

3 Again, lock the lid in place, bring to high pressure. Stabilize the pressure and cook for 20 minutes more. Remove the brisket to a platter and slice on the diagonal to serve. If desired, the pan juices can be thickened by boiling some of the water off and then served over the meat.

Chicken with Lemon and Capers

Ingredients

1/4 cup flour
1 teaspoon salt
1/2 teaspoon freshly ground pepper
4 boneless, skinless chicken breasts
2 tablespoons olive oil
1/2 cup sliced onion
4 ounces sliced mushrooms
1 lemon cut into thick slices
1/4 cup white wine
1/2 cup chicken stock
juice of 1 lemon
1 tablespoon capers, rinsed and drained
1/4 cup minced fresh parsley

Serves 4

Pressure Cooking Time
5 minutes

Directions

1 Combine the flour, salt and pepper. Coat the chicken pieces in the seasoned flour. Heat the olive oil in the pressure cooker and brown the chicken on both sides. Remove the chicken to a platter.

2 In the pressure cooker, add the sliced onion, mushrooms and lemon. Stir in the white wine, stock, lemon juice and rinsed capers. Combine well. Return the chicken pieces to the cooker.

3 Lock the lid in place, bring to high pressure. Stabilize the pressure and cook for 5 minutes. Release the pressure and remove the thick lemon slices. Serve the chicken with the pan gravy and garnish with the minced parsley.

Stephanie's Saltimboca

Fast, easy, and so very elegant.

Ingredients

4 veal cutlets, about 3/4 pound, pounded VERY thin
4 slices prosciutto
4 slices provolone cheese
2 tablespoons olive oil
1/2 cup flour
1/2 teaspoon ground sage
salt and pepper
1 clove garlic, minced
1/2 cup white wine

Serves 4

Pressure Cooking Time

5 minutes

Directions

1   Place the pounded veal on a work surface. Season the meat with salt and pepper. Layer with the prosciutto and then the cheese. Roll up and secure with toothpicks. Repeat with all four pieces. Combine the flour and sage. Dredge the meat rolls in the seasoned flour.

2   Heat the oil in the cooker and add the garlic. Add the meat rolls and brown on all sides. Add the wine. Lock the lid in place, bring to high pressure.

3   Stabilize the pressure and cook for 5 minutes. Release the pressure. Remove the toothpicks and serve immediately.

Chinese Chicken Salad

This chicken salad can be served either warm right after cooking or prepared ahead and served cold. Either way, you will get rave reviews!

Ingredients

1 pound boneless, skinless chicken breasts
1 cup chicken stock
2 cloves garlic, minced
1 1/2 teaspoons minced fresh ginger
1 tablespoon soy sauce
1 tablespoon toasted sesame oil
1/4 creamy peanut butter
3 tablespoons hoisin sauce
1/4 cup chopped peanuts or slivered almonds
1/2 cup diced celery
1/2 cup diced carrots
4 cups shredded romaine lettuce
3 cups shredded Napa cabbage
1 cup chow mein noodles, cooked

Directions

1 In the pressure cooker, combine the chicken stock, garlic, ginger soy sauce and sesame oil. Mix well. Add chicken breasts. Lock the lid in place, bring to high pressure. Stabilize the pressure and cook for 8 minutes. Release the pressure. Remove the chicken to a cutting board and cut into thin strips. Cover and keep warm if desired.

2 Strain the broth from the pan into a measuring cup and add enough water to make 1 cup. Discard the solids. Combine the peanut butter and hoisin sauce with the warm broth and blend well with a whisk to make the dressing.

3 In a large bowl combine the cabbage, lettuce, carrots, celery, peanuts and chicken strips. Pour the dressing over the salad and toss. Garnish with the chow mein noodles just before serving.

Serves 6

Pressure Cooking Time
8 minutes

Pork Tenderloin

One of the fastest entrees for dinner. It's also delicious sliced cold on a sandwich or in a tossed salad.

Ingredients

1 3/4 pounds pork tenderloin
salt and pepper
1 tablespoon olive oil
1/2 cup fresh tangerine juice (see note below)
1/2 cup barbecue sauce
1 teaspoon yellow mustard

Serves 4

Pressure Cooking Time
15 minutes

Directions

Note: If tangerines are unavailable, fresh orange juice can be substituted in a pinch.

1   Season the pork with the salt and pepper. Heat the olive oil in the pressure cooker and brown the tenderloin on all sides, about 5 minutes. Add the fresh tangerine juice, barbecue sauce and mustard.

2   Lock the lid in place, bring to high pressure. Stabilize the pressure and cook for 15 minutes. Release the pressure. Remove the tenderloin to a cutting board and cover with foil. Let the meat rest for 5 minutes. Reduce the pan juices over medium heat until thickened. Slice meat and serve with the sauce.

Pulled Pork

This is wonderful as a main course or as a filling for tacos or enchiladas.

Ingredients

- 2 pounds pork roast
- 4 cloves garlic, peeled
- 1 tablespoon ground cumin
- 1 tablespoon salt
- 2 chipolte peppers in adobo sauce, chopped
- 2 tablespoons adobo sauce, less if a milder spice is desired
- 1/2 cup salsa
- 1/4 cup BBQ sauce

Serves 8

Pressure Cooking Time

70 minutes + 10 minutes

Directions

1   Place the pork, garlic cloves, salt and cumin in the pressure cooker with enough water to barely cover. Cover, lock lid in place and bring to high pressure. Stabilize pressure and cook for 70 minutes. Release pressure and remove all but 1/2 cup of the broth. Add the remaining ingredients.

2   Cover, lock lid in place and bring to high pressure. Stabilize pressure and cook for 10 additional minutes. Remove lid. Using 2 forks, shred the meat, it will fall into strands. Serve.

Easy Creamy Tortilla Dinner

This is a great way to use leftover chicken and can be prepared in advance. Serve with a green salad and flan for an easy dinner.

Ingredients

1 cup diced cooked chicken
1/2 can low sodium cream of chicken soup
1 cup chunky salsa
3 /4 cup grated cheddar cheese, divided
   (1/2 cup and 1/4 cup)
1 small can (4 ounces) diced green chilies
1 teaspoon ground cumin
1 tablespoon adobo sauce
4 flour tortillas

Directions

1 Generously butter a pressure cooker baking dish. In a mixing bowl, combine all the ingredients except the tortillas and the 1/4 cup grated cheese.

2 Starting with a tortilla, layer a tortilla in the prepared dish and add 1/3 of the meat mixture. Continue to layer the tortillas with the 1/3 meat mixture in-between ending with a tortilla on top. Top with the remaining 1/4 cup of grated cheese. Cover tightly with a piece of foil that has been buttered, buttered side facing the cheese to prevent sticking.

3 Place on a trivet in the bottom of the pressure cooker with at least 1 inch of water in the base. Try not to have the water touching the base of the baking dish.

4 Cover, lock lid in place and bring to high pressure. Stabilize pressure and cook for 30 minutes. Release pressure, remove foil and serve with additional salsa if desired.

Serves 4

Pressure Cooking Time
30 minutes

Willie's Chili

Great for a cold winter night or watching a football game. Serve with corn bread. For a vegetarian version, omit the ground turkey.

Ingredients

3 tablespoons olive oil
20 ounces ground turkey breast
1 cup bell pepper, diced
1 cup onion, diced
1 cup carro, diced
1/2 pound diced mushrooms
1 jalapeno pepper, minced
10 ounces prepared salsa
2 chipolte peppers in adobo sauce, chopped
1 tablespoon adobo sauce from peppers,
   (more or less to taste)
1 cup tortilla chips, a large handful
1 tablespoon ground cumin
1/2 teaspoon salt

Garnishes:
diced avocado
grated cheese, (cheddar or pepper jack)
diced green onions
sour cream

Directions

1   Heat the olive oil in the pressure cooker, add the ground turkey, the next 5 ingredients and sauté until the meat is no longer pink. Stir in the remaining ingredients.

2   Lock the lid in place, bring to high pressure. Stabilize the pressure and cook for 15 minutes. Release the pressure and serve with the garnishes.

Serves 4-6

Pressure Cooking Time
15 minutes

Garlic Rosemary Lamb

The gravy is made as the lamb cooks, so there's no extra work.

Ingredients

4 pounds of boneless lamb, cubed
salt and pepper
2 tablespoons olive oil
4 cloves of garlic, minced
3 tablespoons flour
1 1/2 cups vegetable stock
4 sprigs of fresh rosemary
1 cup thickly sliced carrots

Serves 6

Pressure Cooking Time
20 minutes

Directions

1 Generously season the lamb cubes with salt and pepper. Heat the olive oil in the pressure cooker, add the lamb cubes and garlic. Brown the meat on all sides. Stir in the flour, mixing well.

2 Gradually stir in the stock. Add the carrots and rosemary. Lock the lid in place, bring to high pressure. Stabilize the pressure and cook for 20 minutes. Release the pressure. Remove the rosemary stems as the leaves will have fallen off. Adjust seasonings to taste and serve.

Beer Braised Beef Short Ribs

Ingredients

1/4 cup olive oil
2 cloves garlic, minced
4 pound beef short ribs
1 cup diced yellow onion
1/2 pound small whole crimini mushrooms
1/2 pound carrots cut into large chunks
3 sprigs of fresh thyme
salt
pepper
12 ounce bottle of dark beer
1 tablespoon of minced parsley

Serves 4

Pressure Cooking Time
20 minutes

Directions

1   Generously season the short ribs with salt and pepper.
Heat the olive oil in the pressure cooker, add the garlic
and sauté. Add the seasoned short ribs and brown
them on all sides. Add the carrots, onions,
mushrooms, and thyme. Stir in the beer.

2   Lock the lid in place, bring to high pressure. Stabilize
the pressure and cook for 20 minutes. Release the
pressure. Stir in parsley and serve.

Turkey Cutlet Supreme

Elegant enough for company but easy enough for a fast dinner, this recipe takes about 20 minutes start to finish.

Ingredients

1/2 cup flour
1/2 teaspoon salt
1/2 teaspoon freshly ground pepper
1 tablespoon dried parsley
1 pound turkey breast cutlets, about 5
1 cup seasoned bread crumbs
2 eggs beaten with 1/4 cup water
olive oil
1/2 pound sliced mushrooms
1/2 large onion, sliced
1 cup chicken stock or white wine,
   (or 50/50 combination of both)

Directions

1 Combine the flour, salt, pepper and parsley in a flat dish. Place the seasoned bread crumbs in another flat dish. Dredge each cutlet in flour, beaten egg and then seasoned bread crumbs. Set aside.

2 Heat about 2 tablespoons of olive oil in the cooker over medium heat. Brown each breaded cutlet on both sides in heated olive oil, do not crowd the pan. The cutlets do not need to be fully cooked as the cooking will be finished later. More oil may need to be added with each additional batch.

3 Remove the browned cutlets and set aside. Sauté the sliced onions and mushrooms in the cooker. Add oil only if necessary. Stir in 1 tablespoon of the seasoned flour into the sautéed vegetables. Stir in the stock and/or wine. Return the partially cooked cutlets to the cooker by placing them on top of the mushroom mixture.

4 Lock the lid in place, bring to high pressure. Stabilize the pressure and cook for 6 minutes. Release the pressure and serve.

Serves 4

Pressure Cooking Time
6 minutes

vegetables

Pressure cooking is an excellent means of bringing out the best in fresh, frozen and dried vegetables. The short amount of time it takes to pressure cook vegetables, while using a small amount of liquid, helps maintain their flavor, nutritional value and color.

Many vegetables can be pressure cooked in as little as one minute. Use a steamer basket and trivet in order to elevate them above the cooking water.

Remember not to fill cooker over 2/3 full, and in most cases, use the quick release method to bring the pressure down instantly with cold water.

Potato and Green Bean Casserole

Ingredients

3 potatoes, peeled and cut into one inch cubes
3/4 pound green beans
1 tablespoon olive oil
1 medium onion, minced
1 clove garlic, minced
1 green pepper, diced
1 tablespoon minced parsley
Salt and freshly ground pepper
1/2 cup chicken stock

Directions

1 Mix together all ingredients in the pressure cooker.
Close the lid, bring to pressure, stabilize and cook
for 3 minutes. Release pressure using cold-water
release method.

Serves 4

Pressure Cooking Time

3 minutes

Stuffed Tomatoes

Ingredients

6 ripe tomatoes
2 cups low-sodium beef broth
2 teaspoons garlic
1 teaspoon salt
2 teaspoons parsley
1 teaspoon dill
1 large onion, minced
1 pound ground lamb
1 cup white rice (long-grain)
1 cup bread crumbs

Serves 6

Pressure Cooking Time

8 minutes

Directions

1. Slide off top of each tomato; scoop out pulp and juice, leaving tomato shells. Mash pulp and add garlic, beef broth, salt, parsley and dill. Set aside.

2. In pressure cooker, sauté onions in oil for 1 1/2 minutes.

3. Add crumbled ground meat, then rice, stirring one minute, then adding tomato, broth and spice mixture.

4. Close lid, bring to high pressure, stabilize and cook for 8 minutes. Open lid using cold-water release method.

5. Spoon mixture into tomato shells that have been placed in a baking pan. Top with bread crumbs, and drizzle butter over top. Place tomato shells in a preheated broiler and bake until tops are browned, approximately 1 1/2 minutes.

Vegetable Fiesta

Ingredients

1 cup low sodium chicken stock
1 cup tomato sauce
1 cup long grain rice
1 teaspoon olive oil
2 medium sized zucchini or squash, cut into 1/4 inch
   round slices
1/2 pound navy beans
1 small head cabbage (white is preferred), cut into 1
   inch pieces
1/8 teaspoon salt

Serves 4

Pressure Cooking Time
5 minutes + 20 minutes

Directions

1 Add chicken stock, olive oil, tomato sauce, and rice to
   pressure cooker, close lid and bring to high pressure.
   Stabilize and cook for 5 minutes.

2 Release pressure using cold-water release method.
   Open lid and add zucchini or squash, beans, cabbage
   and salt. Close lid, bring to high pressure, stabilize
   and cook for 20 minutes, until cabbage
   is tender.

3 Release pressure using cold-water release method.
   Serve.

Spaghetti Squash

Ingredients

2 spaghetti squash, halved
1 pound Italian sausage, removed from casing
1 cup spaghetti sauce
1 cup mild, thick chunky salsa
2 tablespoons horseradish sauce
2 cups very ripe chopped tomatoes
1 tablespoon minced garlic in olive oil
shredded cheddar cheese

Serves 6

Pressure Cooking Time

14 minutes

Directions

1 Place squash in pressure cooker, cut side down in water to cover.

2 Close lid, bring to high pressure, stabilize and cook for 14 minutes until tender.

3 While squash is cooking, sauté sausage in skillet for 15 minutes under low heat.

4 Once sausage is cooked, add spaghetti sauce, salsa and horseradish, stirring well. Cook on low heat for 5 minutes, then add tomatoes and garlic, bringing to a boil. Set aside and keep hot.

5 Release pressure from cooker, drain and remove squash from shell with a fork.

6 Place on an ovenproof platter, then top the squash with reserved sausage mixture and cheddar cheese. Heat in the 325° F. oven until cheese is melted.

Stuffed Artichokes

Ingredients

4 large artichokes (clip leaf tops and cut
   off stems) reserve stems
2 slices of white bread per artichoke
   (stale bread is the best)
1/2 cup Italian bread crumbs
2 tablespoons olive oil
salt, black pepper and garlic to taste
3 tablespoons Parmesan cheese

Serves 4

Pressure Cooking Time

12 minutes

Directions

1. Take stems from artichokes and peel, then chop in small pieces. Put in large bowl.

2. Cut bread in small pieces and add to stems.

3. Take remaining ingredients and mix together, adding enough water to mixture to hold ingredients together. The more spices added, the tastier the recipe.

4. Wash artichokes and spread center open and put stuffing inside.

5. Put artichokes in pressure cooker with enough water to cover 1/3 of artichokes.

6. Close lid, bring to high pressure, stabilize and cook for 12 minutes. Release pressure, open lid and serve while hot.

Green Beans with Walnuts

Ingredients

1 cup chopped walnuts
2 pounds fresh green beans, washed and trimmed
1 1/2 cups water
1 teaspoon salt
2 tablespoons butter
2 tablespoons canola oil
2 tablespoons minced fresh parsley
ground black pepper to taste

Serves 8

Pressure Cooking Time

3 minutes

Directions

1   Place walnuts on ungreased baking sheet and bake at 350° F for 5-8 minutes. Remove from oven and allow to cool.

2   In pressure cooker, add beans and water, along with salt. Close lid, bring to high pressure, stabilize and cook for 3 minutes. Release pressure using cold-water release method. Open lid and place in bowl. Drain any remaining excess water in pot.

3   In pressure cooker pot, melt butter with oil over high heat. Add beans and toss until heated through, about 3-4 minutes. Season with salt and pepper. Add walnuts and parsley, then toss.

4   Transfer to bowl and serve.

Autumn Stew

Ingredients

1 1/2 cups vegetable stock
1 tablespoon low-sodium soy sauce
1 onion, chopped
1 red bell pepper, diced
4 large garlic cloves, minced
1 15-ounce can chopped tomatoes
1 pound (about 4 cups) butternut squash
1/2 teaspoon oregano
1 1/2 teaspoons chili powder
1/2 teaspoon cumin
1/4 teaspoon black pepper
1 15-ounce can kidney beans
1 1/2 cups fresh or frozen corn

Directions

1 Heat 1/2 cup vegetable stock and soy sauce in pressure cooker pot, then add onion, bell pepper and garlic and cook over medium heat until the onion is translucent and most of the vegetable stock has evaporated.

2 Cut the squash in half and remove seeds, then peel and cut into 1/2-inch cubes.

3 Add squash cubes to onion mixture, along with chopped tomatoes, remaining 1 cup stock, oregano, chili powder, cumin and pepper.

4 Close lid, bring up to high pressure, then lower heat on stove and cook for 4 minutes. Release pressure using cold-water release method.

5 Add kidney beans in their liquid and the corn. Cook without lid on for 5 minutes longer. Serve warm with your favorite bread.

Serves 4

Pressure Cooking Time
4 minutes

Cassoulet of Artichokes and Clams

To make this a one dish dinner, add 1 pound of peeled and cubed potatoes to be cooked with the artichokes.

Ingredients

- 8 small fresh artichokes
- 1 pound clams
- 1 teaspoon bread crumbs
- 1 cup white wine
- 3 cloves garlic, minced
- 1/4 cup minced parsley
- 1/4 cup olive oil
- Salt to taste
- 2 tablespoons lemon juice

Directions

1. Scrub the clams well and put them in a bowl with cold water and 2 tablespoons of salt to help release the grit.

2. Meanwhile, clean the artichokes by removing the tough outer leaves, trimming the tips of the leaves, and cutting off the stems. Slice the artichokes in half and place them with the lemon juice in a casserole with cold water to prevent browning. Set aside.

3. Heat the oil in the pressure cooker over medium heat and add the minced garlic and drained artichokes. Season with a pinch of salt. Sprinkle with breadcrumbs and add the white wine. Cover, lock lid in place and bring to high pressure. Stabilize pressure and cook for 5 minutes. Release the pressure.

4. Rinse and drain the clams and add to the pressure cooker. Return the cooker to the heat, stirring until the clams open, about 5 minutes. Discard any clams that do not open. Adjust the salt, sprinkle with the minced parsley, and serve immediately.

Serves 4

Pressure Cooking Time
5 minutes

Country-Style Salad

The recipe can be made by replacing the chicken breast with smoked ham.

Ingredients

1 whole chicken breast
1/4 pound smoked trout
5 medium potatoes
2 large, firm red tomatoes, peeled and cubed
2 carrots, peeled and sliced
2 ribs celery, sliced
1 large sweet onion, diced
12 stuffed green olives
1/2 cup virgin olive oil
2 tablespoons balsamic vinegar
1 tin of anchovies in olive oil
4 almonds
1 teaspoon dried thyme
2 hard boiled eggs
Salt to taste

Directions

1 Cut the chicken breast in half and grill over medium heat until done. Cut it into thin slices. Cut the smoked trout into bite-sized pieces. Reserve both for later.

2 Put the potatoes, well scrubbed and unpeeled, in the steamer basket of the pressure cooker with 2 cups of water and 1 teaspoon of salt. Cover, lock lid in place and bring to high pressure. Stabilize pressure and cook for 5 minutes. Release the pressure.

3 Peel the potatoes, cut them in 1 inch cubes, and put them in a large bowl. Add the reserved chicken and trout. Add the carrots, celery, chopped tomatoes and diced onion.

4 Make the vinaigrette in a blender or food processor. Puree the olives with the olive oil and vinegar. Add the anchovies, almonds, thyme and the hard boiled eggs and process until smooth. Check seasonings. Pour the vinaigrette over the potato mixture in the bowl. Cover with plastic wrap and chill for 2 hours before serving to allow the potatoes to thoroughly absorb the flavor of the vinaigrette.

Serves 4

Pressure Cooking Time
5 minutes

Wild Asparagus

When asparagus are plentiful, prepare more than needed to be added to salads or eaten plain. Drizzle with olive oil or toasted sesame oil for a delightful salad.

Ingredients

2 bunches green asparagus
1 cup water
1/2 teaspoon salt

Directions

1. Snap off the woody ends of the asparagus spears and use a potato peeler to eliminate the tough outer parts.

2. Put the asparagus in a steamer basket and place the basket in the pressure cooker. Add the 1/2 teaspoon of salt and one cup of water. Cover, lock lid in place and bring to high pressure. Stabilize pressure and cook for 2 minutes. Release the pressure quickly. Drain the asparagus and place on a platter.

3. Serve lukewarm.

Serves 4

Pressure Cooking Time

2 minutes

Asparagus
with Garlic-Browned Tomato

*This is a wonderful salad when the vegetables are fresh
and abundant.*

Ingredients

16 thick white or green asparagus
1 teaspoon sugar
1/2 teaspoon salt
3 large red salad tomatoes cut into 1/2 inch slices
8 thin slices of Serrano ham or prosciutto
2 hard boiled eggs finely minced
2 cloves garlic, minced
1 sprig of parsley, minced
Extra-virgin olive oil
Salt to taste

Directions

1   Snap off the woody ends of the asparagus spears and
peel the exterior portions to remove the tough parts.
Put the asparagus in a steamer basket and place the
basket in the pressure cooker. Add the teaspoon of
sugar, 1/2 teaspoon of salt and one cup of water.
Cover, lock lid in place and bring to high pressure.
Stabilize pressure and cook for 3 minutes. Release the
pressure quickly. Drain the asparagus and place in a
bowl to cool.

2   Heat 2 tablespoons of oil in a skillet and brown the
tomato slices for 1 minute. Flip them over, season with
salt, sprinkle with parsley and garlic, and cook 1
minute more. Remove from skillet and arrange on a
serving platter.

3   Make a tight roll out of each 1/2 slice of ham. Arrange
the ham rolls on the browned tomatoes. In the center
of the platter, arrange the cooled asparagus and
garnish with the finely minced hard boiled eggs.
Drizzle with virgin olive oil. Serve at room temperature.

Serves 4 as an appetizer

Pressure Cooking Time
3 minutes

Spinach with Pine Nuts

This is a lovely way to enjoy fresh spinach. Bags of pre-washed spinach make this a very fast dish. If desired add a few peeled shrimp to the final sauté for a delicious appetizer or light lunch.

Serves 4-6

Pressure Cooking Time
2 minutes

Ingredients

2 pounds spinach
2 tablespoons olive oil
3 tablespoons pine nuts
2 cloves garlic, thinly sliced
Salt

Directions

1   Wash the spinach in plenty of cold water to completely remove any particles of grit. Heat the pressure cooker over medium heat and lightly toast the pine nuts. Remove the pine nuts and set aside for later use.

2   Put 1/2 cup of water in the pressure cooker, place the spinach in the steamer basket, and season with salt. Cover, lock lid in place and bring to high pressure. Stabilize pressure and cook for 2 minutes. Release the pressure quickly.

3   Drain the spinach well but without mashing, to keep the leaves whole. Set aside. Heat the oil in the pressure cooker and brown the garlic cloves over medium heat. When browned, add the reserved spinach and the pine nuts and sauté until warmed through.

Catalan-Style Peas

Fresh peas are delightful this way.

Ingredients

2 pounds fresh peas, in the pod
1 small onion, diced
1 cup fennel, diced
4 oz Serrano ham or prosciutto, diced
1/2 cup white wine
3 tablespoons olive oil
1 teaspoon of sugar
Salt

Directions

1　Shell the peas and set aside. Heat the oil in the pressure cooker and sauté the onion and fennel over medium heat until transparent.

2　Add the diced ham, peas, sugar, white wine, and 1/2 cup water. Season lightly with salt. Cover, lock lid in place and bring to high pressure.

3　Stabilize pressure and cook for 2 minutes. Release the pressure.

Serves 6

Pressure Cooking Time
2 minutes

Fava Beans with Ham

Use the freshest Fava beans you can find.

Ingredients

2 pounds fresh Fava beans in the shell
1 cup diced onion
4 ounces Serrano or prosciutto ham, diced
1/2 cup water
1/4 cup olive oil
Salt to taste

Serves 6

Pressure Cooking Time
2 minutes

Directions

1   Shell the beans and set aside. Heat the oil in the pressure cooker over medium heat and sauté the onion and diced Serrano ham for 5 minutes.

2   Add the shelled beans, water, and salt. Cover, lock lid in place and bring to high pressure. Stabilize pressure and cook for 6 minutes. Release pressure.

3   If necessary, bring back to high pressure for an additional minute or two. If the pan juices are very thin, continue cooking for a few minutes with the lid off, so that the beans end up in a nice sauce.

Spring Ragout

A lovely dinner to signify the beginning of Spring. Be sure the Fava beans are very young and tender, otherwise, omit them.

Ingredients

4 raw artichokes
3 tablespoon olive oil
1 onion, chopped fine
1 clove garlic
1 pound veal (cut into 2 inch pieces)
4 carrots, peeled and cubed
1 tablespoon of flour
1/2 cup white wine
1/2 pound Fresh Fava beans
2 potatoes, peeled and cut into 1/2 inch dice
Salt and pepper

Directions

1   Clean the artichokes by removing the tough outer leaves, trimming the tips of the leaves, and peeling the stalks. Slice the artichokes in half vertically. Cook until soft in lightly salted water. Reserve for later use.

2   Heat oil in the pressure cooker and sauté the minced onion and garlic over medium heat until caramelized. Season with salt & pepper. Add the meat, and lightly brown for a few minutes, then sprinkle the flour over the mixture in the pot. Stir well. Add the carrots and white wine. Adjust the salt and pepper. Cover, lock lid in place and bring to high pressure. Stabilize pressure and cook for 10 minutes. Release the pressure.

3   Shell the beans and add to the stew along with the potatoes. Cover, lock lid in place and bring to high pressure. Stabilize pressure and cook for 5 minutes. Release the pressure.

4   Open the lid and stir in the cooked artichokes to reheat them. The sauce should be well blended but light.

5   Serve by placing 2 artichokes halves on a plate, fill the cavities with the meat and pour the sauce over all.

Serves 4

Pressure Cooking Time
10 minutes + 5 minutes

Tricolor Mold

Serve this elegant mold garnished with a spicy tomato sauce. If prepared ahead of time, it can be reheated by covering with aluminum foil and placing in an oven preheated to 400° F for 15 minutes.

Ingredients

- 10 ounces carrots, peeled and left whole
- 3 sprigs of parsley
- 1/2 small cauliflower, cut into florets
- 3 medium potatoes, whole
- 3 tablespoons butter
- 3 eggs
- 3/4 cup evaporated milk
- 1/4 teaspoon white pepper
- 1/4 teaspoon salt

Directions

1. Place the carrots and the parsley in the bottom of the pressure cooker and cover with water. Season with salt. Position the steamer basket above the carrots, and place the cauliflower and potatoes in the steamer basket. Cover, lock lid in place and bring to high pressure. Stabilize pressure and cook for 5 minutes. Release the pressure.

2. Cut the cauliflower into thick slices. Remove the potatoes and mash them with the parsley and 2 tablespoons butter. Cut 1/2 of the carrots into slices and reserve the other half. Make a purée of the remaining carrots. Keep both the mashed potatoes and carrots warm for later use. Use a ring mold that will fit into the cooker and line it with aluminum foil and butter the foil well with the remaining tablespoon. Place a layer of sliced carrots in the bottom, then one of sliced cauliflower, alternating layers and ending with a layer of carrot.

3. Beat the eggs with the evaporated milk. Season with white pepper and salt. Pour this mixture into the mold and cover with aluminum foil. Add 3 inches of water to the bottom of the pressure cooker, position the trivet, and place the mold on top of it. Cover, lock lid in place and bring to high pressure. Stabilize pressure and cook for 15 minutes. Turn off the heat and let the cooker rest for 15 minutes, the pressure should be released at the end of this time. Remove the mold from the cooker and let it sit for an additional 5 minutes.

4. Unmold onto a round platter. With a pastry bag fitted with a star tip, make a decorative design around the mold with hot mashed potatoes. Pipe rosettes of carrot purée (also hot) on top. Serve immediately.

Serves 6

Pressure Cooking Time
5 minutes + 15 minutes

Spicy Rioja Potatoes

Dried peppers are available in the Hispanic sections of most markets. Choose a mild or spicy variety depending on your preference.

Ingredients

2 dried red peppers
2 pounds potatoes
1/4 cup olive oil
10 ounces fresh chorizo sausage,
   cut into pieces
1 onion, diced fine
1 clove garlic, diced fine
1/2 cup white wine
1 teaspoon cumin
Salt to taste

Directions

1 Remove the stems and seeds from the dried red peppers and put them in warm water and soak until softened. When soft, use a spoon to scrape the pulp from the skin.

2 Peel the potatoes and cut them in large chunks.

3 Heat the oil in the pressure cooker over medium heat and sauté the onion, garlic, and chorizo sausage until the chorizo releases its fat. Remove the pieces of chorizo and reserve for later use.

4 Add the potatoes, pulp from the peppers and wine to the pressure cooker and stir for about 5 minutes. Add water to just cover the potatoes. Adjust the salt and add the cumin. Cover, lock lid in place and bring to high pressure. Stabilize pressure and cook for 5 minutes. Release the pressure. Add the reserved pieces of chorizo to the cooker and boil for 2 minutes, stirring to blend the stock.

5 Let rest for 10 minutes before serving.

Serves 6

Pressure Cooking Time
5 minutes

Potatoes in Green Sauce

The clams make this a full meal. Just add a green salad and bread to round out the menu.

Ingredients

2 pounds clams
3 tablespoon olive oil
1 onion minced
1 clove garlic, minced
2 pounds potatoes, peeled and quartered
1/4 cup minced parsley
1/2 cup white wine
1 cup peas, fresh or frozen
1 cup fresh asparagus tips
Salt

Serves 4

Pressure Cooking Time
5 minutes

Directions

1   Put the clams in cold water with a splash of vinegar or salt so they will release their grit. Do this at least one hour before serving.

2   Heat the oil in the pressure cooker over medium heat and sauté the onion and garlic until transparent. Add the potatoes, minced parsley and white wine. Mix well. Add 2 cups water and 1/2 teaspoon salt. Cover, lock lid in place and bring to high pressure. Stabilize pressure and cook for 5 minutes. Release the pressure.

3   Rinse and drain the clams. Open the cooker and add the clams, peas, and asparagus tips. Cook over medium heat just until the clams open.

Stewed Leeks

After preparing this recipe, you can serve the leeks garnished with a generous sprinkling of cheese and broiled for a few minutes.

Ingredients

12 leeks (white part only)
4 carrots, peeled and cut in half
4 black peppercorns
2 cloves
1/4 cup olive oil
3 tablespoons balsamic vinegar
1 cup water
Salt and pepper to taste

Directions

1 Clean the leeks, removing the outer part and washing well under running water.

2 Put them in the pressure cooker along with the carrots, and remaining ingredients. Cover, lock lid in place and bring to high pressure.

3 Stabilize pressure and cook for 4 minutes. Turn off stove and let sit for about 10 minutes. Release pressure and serve.

Serves 4

Pressure Cooking Time
4 minutes

Mushroom Pâté

Since it has no preservatives, this pâté must be eaten quickly, within 3 days. Keep it in the refrigerator, covered.

Ingredients

8 ounces butter, clarified
8 ounces fresh mushrooms, cleaned and chopped
8 ounces chicken livers, chopped
8 ounces chicken breast meat, chopped
1 lemon
Salt & pepper to taste

Directions

1   Clarify the butter by melting it over low heat in a small pan. Once melted, filter out the solids by straining through cheesecloth placed over a small bowl.

2   In the pressure cooker, over medium heat, place the mushrooms and 1/2 cup water. Season with a pinch of salt. Add the chicken livers and chicken breast. Cover, lock lid in place and bring to high pressure. Stabilize pressure and cook for 2 minutes. Release the pressure naturally.

3   Drain well. Make a smooth paste of the mushrooms, chicken livers, and chicken breast by putting them through a food mill twice and draining off the juices from the mixture. Alternately, a blender or food processor can be used. Add half of the butter, adjust the salt, and add a pinch of pepper and a couple of drops of lemon juice. Puree until smooth.

4   Press the pâté tightly into a ceramic bowl so that there are no air holes. Cover with the remaining butter and let it chill in the refrigerator. Serve with toasted bread and a crisp green salad.

Serves 8 as an appetizer

Pressure Cooking Time
2 minutes

Cauliflower Bouquets

A festive way to present a warm cauliflower salad.

Ingredients

1 small head of cauliflower, cleaned and trimmed
2 medium beets
3 hard boiled eggs, sliced
2 cloves

Dressing:
1 cup olive oil
1/3 cup balsamic vinegar
Salt and pepper to taste

Directions

1 Put 2 cloves and 2 cups of water in the pressure cooker. Cut the cauliflower into florets. Place the cauliflower florets in a steamer basket and place the basket in the pressure cooker. Season with salt. Cover, lock lid in place and bring to high pressure. Stabilize pressure and cook for 3 minutes. Release the pressure. Remove from the cooker and set aside, covered to keep warm.

2 Wash the beets and trim the stems, down to 1/2 inch, and then put them whole into the cooker along with 1 cup water and salt. Cover, lock lid in place and bring to high pressure. Stabilize pressure and cook for 7 minutes. Release pressure and let cool. Drain, peel, and slice. (Alternately, use canned beets that have been rinsed and drained). Slice the hard boiled eggs.

3 Prepare the vinaigrette by mixing the oil, vinegar, salt and pepper to taste in a bowl.

4 On a platter, arrange the sliced beets in an overlapping circle. Place the warm cauliflower florets around the beets and add the sliced cooked eggs in the middle. Sprinkle with the dressing.

Serves 4

Pressure Cooking Time
3 minutes + 7 minutes

Cabbage with Chorizo Sausage

This can be served with steamed new potatoes. Add to the cooked cabbage just before serving.

Ingredients

1 large cabbage
10 oz chorizo sausage, cut in pieces
2 tablespoons olive oil
3 cloves of garlic, minced
Salt to taste
2 cups water

Directions

1 Julienne the cabbage and put it in the pressure cooker along with the chorizo sausage, cut in pieces, 2 cups of water, and salt to taste. Lock the lid in place, bring to high pressure. Stabilize the pressure and cook for 4 minutes. Release the pressure.

2 Drain the cabbage and set aside.

3 Heat the oil in a skillet and brown the cloves of garlic, cut in thin slices. Pour over the cabbage and simmer over medium heat for 15 minutes, stirring frequently.

Serves 4

Pressure Cooking Time
4 minutes

Mediterranean
Vegetable Spread for bread

Ingredients

3 tablespoons olive oil
1/4 teaspoon red pepper flakes
4 cloves garlic, crushed
2 bunches green onions, sliced into 1 inch pieces
1 large red bell pepper, diced
1 medium eggplant, about 3/4 pound, peeled and
    cut into 1 inch cubes
1 14.5 oz can peeled, diced tomatoes in juice
1 teaspoon dried oregano
1/4 teaspoon fresh ground pepper
1/2 cup grated parmesan cheese, divided
1 loaf of French bread, sliced horizontally
fresh basil

Serves 6

Pressure Cooking Time

5 minutes

Directions

1   In the pressure cooker, sauté the red pepper flakes
    and garlic until fragrant. Stir in onion, bell pepper,
    eggplant and cook for 1 minute. Stir in oregano,
    canned tomatoes, and ground pepper. Close lid and
    bring to high pressure. Stabilize pressure and cook
    5 minutes. Release pressure and let cool to room
    temperature.

2   Preheat broiler. Blend in 1/4 cup of the cheese and
    spread the mixture onto each half of the bread.
    Sprinkle the remaining cheese on top. Broil until the
    cheese is bubbling. Remove to cutting board and slice
    diagonally. Garnish with basil if desired.

Millet & Cauliflower
"Mashed Potatoes"

Ingredients

1 cup millet
1 cup chopped cauliflower
1 medium to large onion, chopped
Salt & pepper to taste

Directions

1 Wash millet well; drain. Place in pressure cooker. Add cauliflower, salt, pepper and onion. Add 2 cups water and stir.

2 Bring to a boil; place lid on cooker. Bring to high pressure. Stabilize and cook for 15 minutes. Release pressure and remove lid. Stir to "mash." Serve hot.

Serves 6

Pressure Cooking Time
15 minutes

soups, stocks & stews

For quick, delicious soups that taste like they've been cooking on the stove for hours, nothing cooks soup faster than a pressure cooker. Whether it's bean soup, vegetable soup, creamy bisques, or delicious stocks, pressure cooking enhances the flavor of soups, while retaining up to 50% more vitamins and minerals. So for your good health, cook some soup today. It's excellent whether served alone or with a meal.

Beef Stock

Ingredients

1 tablespoon olive oil

2 pounds stewing beef, such as shanks, cut in 1-inch cubes

1 pound beef bones

8 cups water

1 medium onion, coarsely chopped

1 large carrot, peeled and coarsely chopped

1 bay leaf

Salt to taste

6 peppercorns

1 celery stalk, coarsely chopped

2 sprigs parsley

1/2 teaspoon thyme

Serves 6

Pressure Cooking Time

60 minutes

Directions

1   Heat oil in cooker until very hot, then add beef and bones, as much as will comfortably fit at one time. Cook until well browned. Repeat with remaining beef and bones. Drain off any excess fat.

2   Add remaining ingredients, close lid and bring to high pressure, stabilize and cook for 1 hour. Release pressure and remove lid, then strain, pressing with the back of a wooden spoon to extract as much liquid as possible. Refrigerate overnight and skim the fat from the surface before using.

Chicken Stock

Ingredients

2 pounds chicken pieces
1 teaspoon salt
3/4 pound onions, coarsely chopped
1/4 pound carrots, coarsely chopped
1/4 pound celery, coarsely chopped
3 large springs of parsley
2 garlic cloves, coarsely chopped
1 bay leaf
Pinch of thyme
1/4 teaspoon peppercorns
8 cups of water

Directions

1   In pressure cooker, combine all ingredients.

2   Cover, bring to high pressure. Stabilize pressure and cook for 1 hour.

3   Cool and strain out solids before using.

Serves 6

Pressure Cooking Time
60 minutes

Fish Stock

Ingredients

2 pounds of fish bones (heads and trimmings), coarsely chopped. Remove gills makes the stock bitter.
1 tablespoon of butter
1/2 pound onions, coarsely chopped
1/4 pound celery, coarsely chopped
1/4 pound leeks, coarsely chopped
3 large sprigs of parsley
1 teaspoon salt
1 teaspoon lemon juice
1 clove
1 garlic clove, coarsely chopped
1 bay leaf
Pinch of thyme
1/4 teaspoon peppercorns
8 cups water

Serves 6

Pressure Cooking Time
15 minutes

Directions

1. In pressure cooker, cook fish bones in butter for 5 minutes.

2. Stir in remaining ingredients, except water and sauté until onions are translucent.

3. Add water, cover, bring to high pressure. Stabilize pressure and cook for 15 minutes.

4. Cool and strain out solids before serving.

Potato Leek Soup

Ingredients

6 large Idaho potatoes, cut into 1/2-inch chunks
1 large onion, diced
1 bunch of leeks, cleaned, ends removed, and cut into
1/4-inch slices (white part only, about 1 cup)
4 tablespoons butter
6 cups chicken broth
1 pint half & half

Directions

1   In pressure cooker pot, sauté the potatoes, onion and
    leeks in butter over medium heat. Stir constantly for
    3 minutes. Add chicken broth and close lid.

2   Bring to high pressure, stabilize and cook for 12
    minutes. Release pressure.

3   Open lid and let cool slightly.

4   In blender, puree one half of the soup with half and
    half. Combine with rest of soup mixture and serve.

Serves 6

Pressure Cooking Time
12 minutes

Creamy Corn Chowder

Ingredients

4 slices thick bacon, diced
1 small jalapeño pepper,
  seeded and finely diced
1 cup leek, diced (white part only)
1/2 cup diced red bell pepper
1/2 cup diced carrots
3 cups corn kernels, fresh or frozen
2 cups diced Yukon Gold potatoes
2 cups chicken stock
1/2 teaspoon ground cumin
1 teaspoon chili powder (or more to taste)
salt and pepper
1 tablespoon flour
1/2 cup cream
2 tablespoons minced fresh cilantro

Directions

1 In the pressure cooker, brown the diced bacon over medium heat. Once cooked, drain the bacon and set it aside until later.

2 Leave 2 tablespoons of bacon fat in the pressure cooker. In the reserved bacon fat, sauté the diced leeks, carrots, jalapeño, red bell pepper and corn kernels until the leeks are translucent. Add the cumin and chili powder and mix well. Stir in the potatoes and broth.

3 Lock the lid in place and bring the cooker to high pressure. Stabilize pressure and cook for 10 minutes. Release the pressure. Mix in bacon.

4 In a small bowl, whisk together the flour and cream. Stir this mixture into the soup and cook until thickened. Season with pepper and salt if desired. Garnish with cilantro.

Serves 4

Pressure Cooking Time

10 minutes

Pasta E Fagioli

This wonderful Italian soup is perfect to warm up with on a cool day

Ingredients

1 cup chopped onion
2 cups dried red beans
2 small carrots, grated
1 tablespoon dried parsley
1/2 cup chopped celery
2 teaspoons dried basil
1 clove garlic, minced
1/8 teaspoon ground cayenne pepper
1/4 pound prosciutto, finely chopped
1 tablespoon distilled white vinegar
1 tablespoon olive oil
2 teaspoons white sugar
6 cups tomato juice
1 (16 ounce) package ditalini pasta
3 cups chicken broth or water (to reduce salt content, use water)

Directions

1   In pressure cooker pot, sauté onions, carrots, celery, garlic and prosciutto in olive oil until onion is clear.

2   Add chicken broth, tomato juice, red beans, parsley, basil, red pepper (cayenne), vinegar and sugar. Season, if desired, with salt and pepper.

3   Close lid, bring to high pressure, then lower heat to simmer and cook for 20 minutes.

4   In the meantime, in a separate pot, cook ditalini according to package directions. Cook until tender and drain.

5   When pressure-cooking is done, release pressure.

6   Laddle into separate serving bowls. Leftovers can be frozen if desired.

Serves 12

Pressure Cooking Time
20 minutes

Ratatouille Vegetable Stew

Ingredients

4 tablespoons olive oil
1 small eggplant, peeled and cut into 1-inch cubes
2 medium zucchini, cut in 1/2 inch slices
2 green peppers, seeded and cut in strips
1 medium potato, diced
1 large onion, chopped
2 cloves garlic, minced
2 medium tomatoes, chopped
2 tablespoons parsley, minced
1/4 cup chicken stock

Serves 2-4

Pressure Cooking Time

3 minutes

Directions

1 Heat 2 tablespoons of the oil in the cooker and stir fry the eggplant, zucchini, peppers and potato briefly in small batches. Remove to a warm platter.

2 Add the remaining 2 tablespoons oil and the onion and garlic and sauté slowly until the onion is softened.

3 Return the vegetables to the cooker along with the remaining ingredients.

4 Close the lid and bring to high pressure, stabilize pressure and cook for 3 minutes.

5 Release pressure and remove the lid. Serve with cooked rice on the side.

Everyone's Favorite
Meatball Stew

Ingredients

1 1/2 pounds chopped meat- (either all beef or a
    mixture of beef, pork and veal)
1 egg, lightly beaten
2 slices white bread, soaked in water and squeezed dry
2 tablespoons minced parsley
l/2 teaspoon nutmeg
1 teaspoon Worcestershire sauce
2 cloves garlic, minced
Flour for dusting
2 tablespoons olive oil
3/4 cup fresh or frozen peas
2 carrots, cubed or cut into sticks
2 medium potatoes, peeled and cut in 1 inch cubes
1/2 cup chicken or beef stock (or a mixture of both)
1/4 cup dry white wine
1 bay leaf

Directions

1 In a large bowl combine the chopped meat with the
egg, bread, parsley, nutmeg, Worcerstershire sauce,
garlic, and a tablespoon of stock.

2 Form into 2 inch meatballs and dust lightly with flour,
Heat the oil in the Cooker, add the meatballs and
brown well on all sides. Add the peas, carrots,
potatoes, remaining stock, wine and bay leaf. Close
the cover and bring to pressure.

3 Stabilize pressure and cook for 5 minutes. Release the
pressure and remove the lid. Discard the bay leaf.
Serve with a good crusty bread on the side.

Serves 4

Pressure Cooking Time
5 minutes

Indian Summer Stew

Ingredients

2 tablespoons olive oil
1 medium yellow onion, chopped
1 medium green pepper, chopped
3 medium zucchinis cut into 1/4-inch slices
2 cups frozen corn
1 teaspoon diced jalapeno
2 whole breasts of chicken, cut into 1-inch cubes
2 cups water
1/2 teaspoon cumin
8 ounces sour cream
1 diced red pepper

Serves 4-6

Pressure Cooking Time

5 minutes

Directions

1   Warm oil in cooker. Add onions and garlic and sauté on medium-high heat until opaque.

2   Add chicken and brown lightly.

3   Add remaining ingredients, except sour cream and diced red pepper.

4   Close lid, bring to high pressure, stabilize and cook for 5 minutes. Release pressure. Salt and pepper to taste. Serve in attractive bowls with sour cream and diced red pepper sprinkled on top.

French Onion Soup

Ingredients

5 medium onions, thinly sliced
4 tablespoons butter
6 cups beef or chicken stock, or a mixture of both
1/4 teaspoon freshly ground pepper
2 tablespoons dry white wine or 1 tablespoon dry sherry
6 slices French or Italian bread, lightly toasted
1/2 cup grated parmesan cheese

Directions

1   Melt the butter in the Cooker, add the onion slices and
    cook very slowly for about 20 minutes until golden.

2   Add the stock, pepper and wine, close the lid and
    bring to high pressure. Cook for 15 minutes. Release
    the pressure and remove the lid.

3   Serve in soup bowls with a slice of toasted bread on
    top and sprinkled with the cheese.

Serves 4-6

Pressure Cooking Time
15 minutes

Tortilla Soup

Ingredients

1/3 cup olive oil
2 onions, diced
4 cloves garlic, peeled
1 can (15 oz) tomatoes, drained
12 cups chicken broth
Tortilla chips
Cilantro, chopped (to taste)
1 pound grated cheese
Lime wedges (optional)

Directions

1   Heat oil in cooker, then add onions and garlic cloves. Sauté until deep golden brown.

2   Remove from cooker and puree with tomatoes in blender or food processor until smooth. Return to cooker and add broth. Heat to boiling. Bring up to high pressure, stabilize and cook for 10 minutes. Release pressure and remove the lid.

3   Add cilantro and salt to taste. Place cheese and tortilla chips in individual soup bowls and pour hot soup on top.

4   Serve with lime wedges, if desired.

Serves 8-10

Pressure Cooking Time

10 minutes

162

Traditional Beef Burgundy

For a classic dinner, serve the meat and gravy with steamed potatoes.

Ingredients

4 slices thick bacon, diced
1/4 cup flour
1/2 teaspoon salt
1/2 teaspoon pepper
1/2 teaspoon garlic powder
2 pounds beef, cubed
1 large yellow onion, sliced
3 large carrots, sliced
1 pound mushrooms, quartered
2 cups burgundy wine
1 cup beef stock
1/2 teaspoon dried thyme
1 tablespoon Dijon mustard

Directions

1. In the pressure cooker, brown the diced bacon over medium heat. Once cooked, drain the bacon and set aside until later. Reserve 2 tablespoons of the bacon fat in the pan.

2. Combine the flour, salt, pepper and garlic powder in a small dish. Coat the meat with the seasoned flour. Over medium heat, brown the meat in the reserved bacon fat. Add the quartered mushrooms, carrots and onions to the pan and cook for a minute or two. Stir in the wine, beef stock, mustard and thyme. Lock the lid in place, bring to high pressure.

3. Stabilize the pressure and cook for 30 minutes. Release the pressure, add the reserved bacon and check seasonings. Serve.

Serves 4

Pressure Cooking Time

30 minutes

Lemony Garlic Lamb Stew

Ingredients

- 2 tablespoons olive oil
- 3 pounds lamb stew meat, cut in
  2 inch pieces
- 3 cloves garlic, minced
- 6 tablespoons freshly squeezed
  lemon juice
- 6 tablespoons chicken stock

Directions

1. Heat the oil in the cooker, add the meat (as much as will comfortably fit at one time) and brown well. Season with salt and pepper and stir in the garlic.

2. Add the lemon juice and stock, close the lid and bring to pressure over medium heat. Cook for the suggested time.

3. Release pressure and remove the lid. Serve with noodles or other pasta sprinkled with grated cheese.

Serves 4

Pressure Cooking Time

20 minutes

Greek Style Lentil Soup

Ingredients

2 tablespoons olive oil
2 medium onions, chopped
3/4 pound lentils, washed
6 cups water
15 oz. can whole tomatoes
4 cloves garlic, unpeeled ·
1 bay leaf
1/2 teaspoon crushed allspice
6 tablespoons vinegar
4 precooked Italian sausage (optional)
Salt, freshly ground pepper
4 small whole red potatoes, peeled

Serves 4

Pressure Cooking Time
8 minutes + 7 minutes

Directions

1   Heat the oil in the cooker and sauté the onion until translucent. Stir in the lentils and sauté 10 minutes more. Add the water, close the lid and bring to high pressure. Stabilize and cook for 8 minutes.

2   Release pressure and remove the lid. Add the tomato, garlic, bay leaf, allspice, vinegar, sausage, salt, pepper and potatoes. Close the lid and lock in place.

3   Bring unit back up to high pressure and complete cooking for 7 minutes. Release pressure and remove the lid. Discard the bay leaf and serve.

Shrimp Bisque

The next time you cook shrimp, freeze the shells to make this delicate soup at a later date.

Ingredients

3 tablespoons unsalted butter
1 tablespoon olive oil
1/2 pound of shrimp shells (from
    about 2 pounds of shrimp)
2 large carrots, diced
1 cup diced celery
8 oz shallots, diced
1 clove garlic
1 tablespoon whole peppercorns
1/2 teaspoon thyme
1 tablespoon brandy
6 cups vegetable stock
2 tablespoon unsalted butter
1/4 cup flour
1/4 pound shrimp meat cut into
    1/2 inch pieces
1 cup half and half
Fresh parsley sprigs

Directions

1 In the pressure cooker, over medium heat melt 1 tablespoon of butter and 1 tablespoon of olive oil.

2 Sauté the shrimp shells until bright pink. Stir in the carrots, celery, shallots, garlic, thyme, peppercorns, brandy and vegetable stock. Lock the lid in place, bring to high pressure. Stabilize the pressure and cook for 20 minutes. Release the pressure.

3 Strain the contents of the pressure cooker through a fine mesh strainer into a bowl and discard the shells. In the bottom of the cooker, melt 2 remaining tablespoons of butter and stir in the 1/4 cup of flour.

4 Gradually stir in the strained broth. Keeping the heat low, add the shrimp meat and stir until it is cooked through. Check seasonings, and add salt if desired. Stir in the half and half.

5 Serve, garnished with a sprig of fresh parsley.

Serves 6

Pressure Cooking Time
20 minutes

Fresh Vegetable Soup

This is a light soup that makes a great first course or a simple lunch. Try to cut the vegetables in uniform sizes for even cooking

Ingredients

- 1 tablespoon olive oil
- 3 cloves garlic, minced
- 2 cups diced sweet yellow onion
- 1 1/2 cups diced carrots
- 1 1/2 cup fresh green beans
- 8 oz chopped fresh spinach
- 1 pound peeled and diced fresh tomatoes or 1 (14.5 oz) can diced tomatoes, undrained
- 1 tablespoon dried basil
- 1 teaspoon dried oregano
- 1/2 teaspoon salt
- 1/2 teaspoon fresh ground pepper
- 4 cup low sodium chicken stock
- 2 cups water

Garnish:
parmesan cheese

Serves 6

Pressure Cooking Time
10 minutes

Directions

1. Heat the oil in the pressure cooker over medium heat and sauté the garlic and onion until fragrant, about one minute. Stir in the remaining ingredients. Lock the lid in place, bring to high pressure.

2. Stabilize the pressure and cook for 10 minutes. Release the pressure. Check seasonings and serve with a sprinkling of parmesan cheese.

Cream of Mushroom Soup

This is a delightful soup that features the subtle flavors of the mushroom.

Ingredients

1/2 cup chopped shallots
1 1/2 pounds chopped mushrooms (see note below)
3 Tablespoons olive oil
1/2 teaspoon salt
1/2 teaspoon freshly ground pepper
Generous pinch of dried thyme
2 cups chicken stock
2 tablespoons cornstarch
2 cups milk
1 cup half and half

NOTE: Any type of mushrooms can be used. Portobello mushrooms are a delicious choice, but the dark brown gills on the underside must be removed before cooking or the soup will have a muddy appearance.

Directions

1   Heat the olive oil in the cooker and sauté the shallots and mushrooms until very soft. Season with the salt, pepper and thyme. Stir in the chicken stock. Lock the lid in place, bring to high pressure. Stabilize the pressure and cook for 5 minutes. Release the pressure.

2   In a blender, puree the mushroom mixture until smooth. Whisk the cornstarch into the pressure cooker with the 2 cups of cold milk. Stir the mushroom mixture in, and cook for a few minutes until slightly thickened.

3   Remove from heat and stir in the half and half. Serve. (optional: A drizzle of truffle oil can be added.)

Serves 4

Pressure Cooking Time
5 minutes

Broccoli Vegetable
Cheese Soup

Ingredients

- 1 cup water
- 2 large fresh broccoli, (whole broccoli), chopped into 1/4 inch chunks
- 1 medium zucchini squash (or 2 small), cut into 1/4 inch chunks
- 1 bunch spinach, chopped (or one box frozen chopped spinach)
- 2 cans condensed cheddar cheese soup
- Salt and pepper to taste

Serves 4

Pressure Cooking Time

5 minutes + 10 minutes

Directions

1. Place all ingredients, except condensed cheese soup, into pressure cooker, bring up to high pressure. Stabilize pressure cook for 5 minutes.

2. Release pressure, open cooker and add condensed cheddar cheese soup. Stir.

3. Place lid back on cooker and bring back up to high pressure, stabilize heat and cook additional 10 minutes.

4. Release pressure.

Asparagus Soup

Fresh asparagus usually signals the beginning of Spring. Omit the half and half for a lighter soup with a healthy asparagus flavor or leave it in for a delicate starter for a springtime dinner

Serves 4

Pressure Cooking Time
10 minutes

Ingredients

1 1/2 pounds fresh asparagus
2 tablespoons unsalted butter
1 cup (5 oz.) minced shallots
Pinch of thyme
14 oz low sodium chicken stock
salt and pepper to taste
1 cup half and half

Directions

1. Clean the asparagus and trim off any tough stems. Cut the asparagus into 2 inch pieces. In the pressure cooker over medium heat, lightly sauté the shallots in the butter, being very careful not to burn the butter. Stir in the prepared asparagus, thyme, stock and lightly season with the salt and pepper.

2. Lock the lid in place, bring to high pressure. Stabilize the pressure and cook for 10 minutes. Release the pressure.

3. In batches, puree the soup in a blender until smooth. Return to pan, adjust seasonings and stir in the half and half. Serve with a garnish of fresh thyme.

Ruddy Onion Soup

Ingredients

7 cups yellow onions
2 teaspoons garlic, minced
2 cups vegetable stock or water
1/2 cup dry sherry
1/2 cup dry vermouth
1 tablespoon olive oil
1 tablespoon flour
2 tablespoons tomato sauce
2 tablespoons soy sauce
1/4 cup scallion tops, minced

Directions

1 Slice the onions into 1/4 inch thick rounds, then cut them into half-rounds and set aside.

2 In pressure cooker, add the olive oil and flour, turn on stove to medium flame, and stir to form a paste. Cook until it turns a bit brown, 3-5 minutes.

3 Add the onions and garlic and sauté while stirring continuously 5 minutes, until the onion edges begin to soften.

4 Add stock or water, sherry, vermouth and tomato sauce.

5 Put on lid, bring up to high pressure, stabilize and cook for 4 minutes. Release pressure.

6 Season with soy sauce. Taste and adjust the seasoning if needed. Add the scallion tops. If you wish a thinner soup, add more stock or water.

Serves 4

Pressure Cooking Time

4 minutes

Manhattan Clam Chowder

Ingredients

4 slices bacon, diced
1 medium onion, finely chopped
1 clove garlic, minced
1/4 cup diced green pepper
1 tablespoon flour
1 large potato, diced
1/4 cup finely chopped celery
14 ounce can whole tomatoes, chopped
2 1/2 cups clam juice, fish stock, or water
1 bay leaf
Salt and freshly ground pepper to taste
1 cup minced clams, canned

Serves 4

Pressure Cooking Time

5 minutes

Directions

1   Sauté the bacon in the cooker until it begins to
    brown.

2   Add the onion, garlic and green pepper and cook
    until the green pepper is softened. Stir in the flour,
    then add the potato, celery, tomato, clam juice,
    bay leaf, salt and pepper. Close the lid and bring
    to high pressure.

3   Stabilize and cook for 5 minutes. Release the pressure
    and open the cooker. Discard the bay leaf. Stir in the
    clams and serve.

4   The soup gains in flavor if it sits a few hours at room
    temperature before serving or is refrigerated
    overnight.

Greek Tomato Soup

Ingredients

2 pound piece of beef suitable for soup,
   such as chuck
2 beef knuckle bones
4 cups water
Salt, freshly ground pepper to taste
3 cups crushed tomato
1 celery stalk
2 large carrots, peeled
1 leek, very well washed
2 springs parsley
4 small red potatoes, well scrubbed,
   skin on
2 cups very fine noodles
   (about 1/4 pound)
Grated Parmesan cheese

Directions

1 Place the beef (in one piece) and the bones in the cooker. Pour in the water, salt and pepper. Close the lid, bring to high pressure, stabilize and cook for 10 minutes. Release the pressure and remove the lid.

2 Add all the remaining ingredients except the noodles and cheese (remove the bones if the cooker is too full). Close the lid, bring to pressure and complete cooking for 10 more minutes. Meanwhile, bring salted water to a boil in a saucepan and add the noodles. Cook briefly until just done. Drain and reserve.

3 Release the pressure and remove the lid from the cooker. Transfer the meat, potatoes, carrots, leek and celery to a warm platter. Discard the bones. Strain the remaining liquid into a bowl or container and add the meat and vegetables.

4 Mix the noodles into the soup and serve with grated cheese as a garnish.

Serves 4

Pressure Cooking Time
10 minutes + 10 minutes

Vegetable Stew

To make this into a hearty dinner, add 1 pound of lean lamb as you sauté the onion and garlic.

Ingredients

4 raw artichokes
1 tablespoon lemon juice
1/4 cup olive oil
4 cloves garlic, minced
1 large onion, diced
1/4 pound Serrano ham or prosciutto, diced
1/2 pound green beans, cut into 1 inch pieces
4 carrots, peeled and cut into 1 inch chunks
4 zucchini, cut into 1 inch chunks
2 celery ribs, cut into 1 inch chunks
1/2 cup white wine
1 cup broth (chicken or beef)
1 tablespoon of sweet paprika
2 teaspoon dried thyme
1 cup peas, fresh or frozen
2 hard-boiled eggs, finely minced (optional)

Directions

1 Clean the artichokes by removing the tough outer leaves, trimming the tips of the leaves, and peeling the stalks. Slice the artichokes in half vertically. Place them with the lemon juice in a casserole with cold water to prevent browning. Set aside.

2 Heat the oil in the pressure cooker over medium heat and sauté the garlic, onion and ham until the onion is transparent, but without allowing it to brown. Add the reserved artichokes, carrots, green beans, zucchini and celery. Stir in the white wine, broth, thyme and paprika. Season with salt if needed. Cover, lock lid in place and bring to high pressure. Stabilize pressure and cook for 5 minutes. Release the pressure gradually. Add the peas and hard-boiled eggs if desired.

3 Cook for a few minutes over medium heat in the pressure cooker without the lid on, stirring the stock until it is well blended. Adjust salt to taste.

Serves 6

Pressure Cooking Time
5 minutes

Cream of Broccoli Soup

Ingredients

3 tablespoons olive oil

1 large onion

6 medium potatoes peeled & cubed

1 pound broccoli

2 32-ounce cans chicken broth

2 teaspoons thyme

Salt & pepper to taste

1 cup milk or half & half

Directions

1 Wash and trim broccoli florets. In pressure cooker, sauté onion in olive oil for 3 minutes. Add potatoes & broccoli continue to sauté for an additional 3 minutes. Add broth and thyme. Close lid, bring to high-pressure, stabilize pressure and cook 12 minutes. Remove from heat and release pressure.

2 Open lid when ready. Add salt and pepper to taste. Let cool slightly. Puree in blender adding milk or half & half until smooth and creamy. Serve hot.

Serves 6

Pressure Cooking Time

12 minutes

canning

Home canning is a method of preserving food that provides us with a gratifying method for producing some of our favorite recipes. Canning our recipes enable us to store them and enjoy for ourselves or give as gifts to friends & loved ones. Understanding the basic steps for preparation and right equipment are all you need to create a fabulous array of provisions to stock in your pantry. Once the method has been mastered, most people find that canning is one of the most simple and rewarding ways to ensure having your favorite fruits, vegetables, and even meats year- round.

Although canning food at home has traditionally been associated with pastoral residents, it has now begun to emerge as a new trend in greater populated areas. Families in suburban towns as well as urban dwellers are educating themselves on the methods of canning. These basic guidelines will allow you to learn how to can your most favorite recipes with pride.

Why can foods?

Canning can be a safe and cost-effective way to preserve quality food at home. It is an important, safe method of food preservation if practiced properly. The canning process involves placing foods in jars and heating them to a temperature that destroys microorganisms that could be a health hazard or cause the food to spoil. Air is driven from the jar during heating, and as it cools, a vacuum seal is formed. The vacuum seal prevents air from getting back into the product, protecting it from microorganisms that could recontaminate the food.

Before you begin:

Basic Equipment for Canning

PRESSURE CANNER (Fagor 10 qt models are designed for pressure canning)

CANNING RACK

JAR LIFTER

LADLE

BUBBLE FREER

TIMER

JAR WRENCH

MAGNETIC LID WAND

WIDE MOUTH FUNNEL

GLASS JARS- Use only standard home canning jars. Also commonly referred to as 'Mason Jars'

CANNING LIDS –these flat metal lids with sealing compound and a metal screw band are the most popular type of lid for home-canned products.

For more information about Fagor's seven piece HOME CANNING KIT with bonus COOKBOOK sold separately:
Please call 1-800-207-0806 , M-F 9-5 pm EST. or shop online at **www.fagoramerica.com**

1 Jar selection, Preparation and Use:

Examine jars and discard those with nicks, cracks and rough edges. These defects will not permit an airtight seal on the jar, and food spoilage will result. All canning jars should be washed in soapy water, rinsed well and then kept hot before use. This could be done in the dishwasher or by placing the jars in hot water in a pot over a low flame. The jars need to be kept hot to prevent breakage when they're filled with a hot product and placed in the canner for processing.

Using a Pressure Cooker at High Altitudes

The recipes in this cookbook were developed and tested at sea level. Since water and cooking liquids come to a boil more slowly at high altitudes, the cooking times must be longer. A good rule of thumb is to increase the cooking time by 5% for every 1,000 feet above the first 2,000 feet (3,000 feet above sea level, add 5% to cooking time; 4,000 feet, add 10%, and so on).

Since the cooking times increase at altitudes higher than 2,000 feet, you will also have to add more cooking liquid to compensate. There are no fixed rules, so try increasing the cooking liquid by approximately half the percentage of the additional cooking time. For example, if the cooking time is increased by 10%, increase the cooking liquid by 5%.*

2 Lid selection, Preparation and Use:

The common self-sealing lid consists of a flat metal lid held in place by a metal screw band during processing. The flat lid is crimped around its bottom edge to form a trough, which is filled with a colored gasket material. When jars are processed, the lid gasket softens and flows slightly to cover the jar-sealing surface, yet allows air to escape from the jar.

It is best to buy only the quantity of lids you will use in a year. Never reuse lids.

To ensure a good seal, carefully follow the manufacturer's directions in preparing lids for use. Examine all metal lids carefully. Do not use old, dented, or deformed lids or lids with gaps or other defects in the sealing gasket.

Follow the manufacturer's guidelines enclosed with or on the box for tightening the jar lids properly. If screw bands are too tight, air cannot vent during processing, and food will discolor during storage.

Over-tightening also may cause lids to buckle and jars to break, especially with pressure-processed food.

If screw bands are too loose, liquid may escape from jars during processing, seals may fail, and the food will need to be reprocessed.

Do not retighten lids after processing jars. As jars cool, the contents in the jar contract, pulling the self-sealing lid firmly against the jar to form a high vacuum.

Screw bands are not needed on stored jars. They can be removed easily after jars are cooled. When removed, washed, dried, and stored in a dry area, screw bands may be used many times. If left on stored jars, they become difficult to remove, often rust, and may not work properly again.

3 Canning Methods:

There are two safe ways of canning, depending on the type of food being canned. These are the pressure canning method and the boiling water bath method. However, all recipes in this book call for the Pressure Canning method.

*This excerpt was taken from "The Ultimate Pressure Cooker Cookbook" by Tom Lacalamita, page 28.

Pressure Canning Method:

Pressure canning is the only safe method of canning low-acid foods (those with a ph of more than 4.6). Although high acid foods may be canned in either a pressure canner or boiling water bath, pressure canning is the only recommended method for canning low-acid foods. Some low-acid foods include vegetables, meats, poultry and seafood. This method is also necessary for canning such items as soups, stews and chili.

Note: Although considered fruit, tomatoes have a ph value close to 4.6. Therefore you should typically process them in a pressure canner.

Jars of food are placed in 2 to 3 inches of water in a pressure cooker and heated to a temperature of at least 240 °F or above for the correct length of time. Note: This temperature can only be reached in a pressure cooker/canner. Never attempt to can low-acid foods using the water bath method.

Steps for Pressure Canning

Processing Instructions:

- Fill the jars. Allow the proper headspace according to processing directions for specific foods. This is necessary so that all the extra air will be removed during processing, and a tight vacuum seal will be formed.

- To make sure that air bubbles have not been trapped inside the jar, run a bubble freer around the edges of the jar, gently shifting the food, so that any trapped air is released. After the air bubbles have been removed, more liquid may need to be added to the jar to ensure proper headspace.

- Wipe off the rims of the jars with a clean, damp cloth.

- Cap and seal the lids, but not too tightly — air needs to escape during processing. Set the jars of food on the rack in the canner so steam can flow around each jar. Add more boiling water or take out some as needed so that the jars of food are placed in 2 to 3 inches of water (If you add more water, pour it between the jars, not directly on them, to prevent breakage.) Put the lid on the cooker.

- Keep the pressure constant by regulating the heat under the canner. Keep drafts from blowing on the canner. Fluctuating pressure causes loss of liquid from jars and under-processing.

- When the processing is completed, carefully remove the canner from the heat. If the canner is too heavy, simply turn it off.

- Let the pressure in the canner drop to zero using the natural release method. Do not use the cold water or automatic pressure release method for pressure canning.

- When the canner is depressurized, unlock and open the lid.

- Use a jar lifter to carefully remove the jars from the canner. Place the hot jars on a rack, dry towels, boards or newspaper, right side up to prevent the jars from breaking on contact with a cold surface.

- Leave at least 1 inch of space between the jars to cool.

- Do not tighten the lids. Allow the jars to cool, untouched for 12 to 24 hours.

Selecting the Correct Processing Time

To destroy microorganisms in low-acid foods processed with a pressure cooker, you must:

Process the jars for the correct number of minutes at suggested setting. Allow cooker to cool at room temperature using the natural release method until it is completely depressurized.

NOTE: The food may spoil if you fail to use the proper processing times, process at lower pressure than specified, process for fewer minutes than specified, or cool the pressure cooker with water. Remember to adjust timing if you live above sea level.

 4 Finishing Touches

Testing the Lid for a Proper Seal:

Most two-piece lids will seal with a "pop" sound while they're cooling. When it is completely cool, test the lid. It should be curved downward and should not move when pressed with a finger. If a jar is not sealed, refrigerate it and use the unspoiled food within two to three days or freeze it. If liquid has been lost from sealed jars, do not open them to replace it, simply plan to use these first. The food may discolor, but if sealed, the food is safe.

Unsealed Jars: What to Do

If a lid fails to seal, you must reprocess within 24 hours. Remove the lid, and check the jar-sealing surface for tiny nicks. If necessary, change the jar. Always use a new, properly prepared lid, and reprocess using the same processing time.

Instead of reprocessing, unsealed jars of food also can be frozen. Transfer food to a freezer-safe container and freeze. Single, unsealed jars can be refrigerated and used within several days.

Always Inspect Canned Food Before Consuming:

Just as you would avoid a foul smelling, leaking or opened jar of food at the supermarket, don't taste or use home canned food that shows any sign of spoilage. Examine all jars before opening them. A bulging lid or leaking jar is almost always a sure sign of spoilage. When you open the jar, look for other signs such as spurting liquid, unusual odor or mold.

Sterilization of empty jars

To sterilize empty jars, put them right side up on the rack in a boiling-water bath. Fill the bath and jars with hot (not boiling) water to 1 inch above the tops of the jars. Boil 10 minutes. Remove and drain hot sterilized jars one at a time.

Label and Store Jars:

The screw bands should be removed with a jar wrench from the sealed jars to prevent them from rusting on. The screw bands should then be washed, dried and stored for later use.

Store finished product in a clean, cool, dark, dry place. The best temperature is between 50 and 70°F. Avoid storing canned foods in a warm place near hot pipes, a range or a furnace, or in direct sunlight. They lose quality in a few weeks or months, depending on the temperature and may even spoil. Keep canned goods dry. Dampness may corrode metal lids and cause leakage so food will spoil. For best quality, use most canned foods within six months to one year, depending on the recipe.

Home Canning
with your Pressure Cooker

Sweet Pepper and Onion Relish

Ingredients

3 sweet red peppers, medium size, coarsely chopped

3 sweet yellow peppers, medium size, coarsely chopped

4 large white sweet onions, coarsely chopped

1 or 2 very finely chopped jalapeno peppers

7/8 cup sugar

7/8 cup apple cider vinegar

1 1/4 tablespoons salt

Directions

1   Place all ingredients in a large pot. Stir to blend
    thoroughly. Bring to a low boil. Reduce heat and
    simmer for 30 minutes.

2   Ladle into jars, leaving 1/2 inch head space. Cap and
    seal. Place in pressure canner on canning rack in 2-3
    inches of water. Lock lid in place and process for
    20 minutes at high pressure. Let the pressure drop
    using the natural release method.

Servings: 4 pint jars

Headspace: 1 inch

Pressure Cooking Time
20 minutes / High Pressure

Carrots with Mint

Ingredients

2 pounds small carrots
4 cloves of garlic
4 sprigs of fresh mint
4 teaspoons of fresh lemon juice
2 1/2 teaspoons of salt

Directions

1   Wash peel and chop the carrots down to the same size in order to stand vertically in the jars. Fill the jars with equal amounts of carrot, garlic, mint lemon juice and salt.

2   Fill the rest of the jar with boiling water leaving 1/2 inch of headspace. Cap and seal. Place in pressure canner on canning rack in 2-3 inches of water.

3   Lock lid in place and process for 30 minutes at high pressure. Let the pressure drop using the natural release method.

Servings: 4 pints

Headspace: 1/2 inch

Pressure Cooking Time

30 minutes / High Pressure

Chile con Carne

Ingredients

1 1/4 cups dried red kidney beans
2 1/4 cups water
2 teaspoons salt
1 1/4 pounds ground beef
1 small chopped onion
1 small chopped pepper
1/4 teaspoon black pepper
2-3 tablespoons chili powder
3 1/4 cups crushed tomatoes
Salt & pepper to taste

Directions

1. Wash beans thoroughly and place them in a 2qt saucepan. Add cold water to a level of 2 – 3 inches above the beans and soak overnight. Drain and discard water.

2. Combine beans with water and lightly season with salt & pepper. Bring to a boil. Reduce heat and simmer for 30 minutes. Drain and discard water. In a separate skillet, brown ground beef, onions, and peppers. Drain off fat and add to beans with remainder of ingredients. Add 1 cup of water.

3. Simmer for an additional 5-10 minutes. Laddle chile into jars. Cap and seal. Place in pressure canner on canning rack in 2-3 inches of water.

4. Lock lid in place and process for 90 minutes at high pressure. Let the pressure drop using the natural release method.

Servings: 4 pints

Headspace: 1 inch

Pressure Cooking Time
90 minutes / High Pressure

Roasted Peppers

Ingredients

3 green bell peppers
5 red bell peppers
4 yellow bell peppers
2 teaspoons salt
4 cloves garlic
1/3 cup white vinegar
   (4 1/2 teaspoons per jar)
8 sprigs fresh tarragon

Servings: 4 pints

Headspace: 1/2 inch

Pressure Cooking Time
20 minutes / High Pressure

Directions

1. Preheat oven to 400°F. Put the peppers on a baking sheet. Place in the oven, turning frequently, until they begin to turn black and the skin becomes blistered. Remove from oven, peel the peppers and cut them in 1/2. Scrape out the seeds and pulp.

2. Chop peppers into strips. Put the peppers in a strainer and submerge in a saucepan of boiling water for 2-3 minutes. Remove and immediately plunge into cold water.

3. Fill each jar with equal portions of peppers, garlic, vinegar, tarragon and salt. Fill the rest of the jar with boiling water leaving 1/2 inch of headspace. Cap and seal. Place in pressure canner on canning rack in 2-3 inches of water.

4. Lock lid in place and process for 20 minutes at high pressure. Let the pressure drop using the natural release method.

Strawberry Jam

Ingredients

5 cups crushed strawberries
7 cups sugar
1/2 teaspoon margarine
1 package pectin (1 3/4 ounces)

Servings: 4 pints

Headspace: 1/4 inch

Pressure Cooking Time
10 minutes / High Pressure

Directions

1   Wash strawberries and remove stems. Chop & crush in food processor or by hand. In a large pot, measure 5 cups of crushed strawberries. Add margarine and pectin and stir.

2   Bring to a full rolling boil over high heat, stirring constantly. Add sugar to strawberry mixture. Bring to a full, rolling boil again, then boil 1 minute, stirring constantly. Remove from heat; skim off foam.

3   Ladle into clean jars to 1/4 inch from top. Cap and seal. Place in pressure canner in 2-3 inches of water.

4   Lock lid in place and process for 10 minutes at high pressure. Let the pressure drop using the natural release method.

Spicy Creole Tomato Soup

Ingredients

4 pounds tomatoes, peeled, cored and chopped
3 sprigs parsley, stems removed
2 onions, peeled and cut into eighths
2 stalks celery, cut into 2-inch pieces
2 bay leaves
3 garlic cloves, peeled and cut into chunks
1/4 cup margarine
1 tablespoon Creole seasoning mix
2 tablespoons mixed spices tied in cheesecloth
2 tablespoons cup packed brown sugar
1/4 cup flour
1/4 cup water

Directions

1. Combine the first six ingredients and mixed spices in a very large stockpot and cook until all the vegetables are very soft. Remove bay leaves and spice bag.

2. Working in batches, puree the cooked mixture in a blender. To remove seeds and skins, run each blended batch through a food mill. Return the puree to the stockpot and add the margarine, Creole seasoning mix, mixed spices, and brown sugar. In a small bowl, whisk together the flour and water to make a thin paste. Add the paste slowly to the stockpot contents, stirring with the whisk as you do.

3. Bring the soup to a boil and cook until it thickens. Ladle into jars. Cap and seal. Place in pressure canner on canning rack in 2-3 inches of water.

4. Lock lid in place and process for 40 minutes at high pressure. Let the pressure drop using the natural release method.

Servings: 4 pints

Headspace: 1 inch

Pressure Cooking Time
40 minutes / High Pressure

Tomato Lentil and Bean Soup

Ingredients

1 cup black beans
1 cup lentils
2 tablespoons olive oil
1 teaspoon salt
1 onion, peeled and chopped
3 pounds tomatoes, peeled chopped and cored
1/4 cup distilled white vinegar
2 tablespoons sugar
1 1/2 teaspoons Creole seasoning (optional)

Directions

1 Place the black beans and lentils in separate saucepans, cover with water, and soak overnight. To each pan, add 1 teaspoon olive oil and 1/2 teaspoon of salt. Boil until soft. In a stockpot, sauté the onions in the remaining olive oil. Add the tomatoes and cook until soft.

2 Then blend the onion and tomato with a hand-mixer in order to break up the tomatoes. Drain and rinse the black beans and them to the tomatoes mixture. Don't drain the lentils; just add them to the stockpot along with their liquid. Add the vinegar, sugar, and Creole seasoning mix. bring to a boil and cook for 5 minutes before ladling into jars.

3 Cap and seal. Place in pressure canner on canning rack in 2-3 inches of water.

4 Lock lid in place and process for 90 minutes at high pressure. Let the pressure drop using the natural release method.

Servings: 4 pints

Headspace: 1 inch

Pressure Cooking Time
90 minutes / High Pressure

Kalamata Olive Salsa

Ingredients

1 1/2 pounds pitted, chopped Kalamata olives
1 pound pitted, chopped large green olives
3 cups seeded, chopped sweet green peppers
2 cups sun-dried tomatoes, broken into pieces
4 teaspoons dried oregano
4 tablespoons chopped fresh basil
6 garlic cloves, peeled and minced
4 tablespoons balsamic vinegar
4 tablespoons distilled white vinegar
2 cups olive oil
12 crushed black peppercorns

Servings: 4 pints

Headspace: 1/2 inch

Pressure Cooking Time
35 minutes / High Pressure

Directions

1   Combine all the ingredients in a large saucepan and bring to a boil. Turn down the heat and simmer for 30 minutes or until thick before ladling into jars.

2   Be sure that the oil covers the top of the salsa with at least 1/2 inch of headspace. Cap and seal. Place in pressure canner on canning rack in 2-3 inches of water.

3   Lock lid in place and process for 35 minutes at high pressure. Let the pressure drop using the natural release method.

Sweet and Spicy
Seafood Sauce

Ingredients

3 ripe mangos, peeled, pitted, and chopped
3 papayas, peeled, seeded, and chopped
3 jalapeno peppers, seeded and chopped
2 1/4 tablespoons peeled, minced ginger root
1 1/2 oranges, peeled, membranes removed, seeded, and chopped
1 2/3 cups pineapple juice
3 tablespoons lime juice
5 1/2 teaspoons distilled white vinegar
1 teaspoon salt

Servings: 4 pints

Headspace: 1 inch

Pressure Cooking Time
40 minutes / High Pressure

Directions

1   Combine all ingredients in a large saucepan and bring to a boil. Turn down the heat and simmer for 20 minutes or until thick before ladling into jars.

2   Cap and seal. Place in pressure canner on canning rack in 2-3 inches of water.

3   Lock lid in place and process for 90 minutes at high pressure. Let the pressure drop using the natural release method.

Chicken a la king

Ingredients

1 stewing chicken (around 5 pounds)
4 stalks celery, coarsely chopped
1 carrot, peeled and cut into 1 inch chunks
1 medium onion, chopped
1 1/2 teaspoons salt
2 bay leaves
4 whole black peppercorns
2 whole allspice
1/4 cup of butter or margarine
1/2 cup flour
1/2 red bell pepper, seeded and chopped
1 tablespoon chopped fresh parsley
1 teaspoon salt

Directions

1   Place the chicken, 2 stalks of celery, carrot, onion, salt, bay leaves, peppercorns, and allspice in a stew pan. Add water to cover. Cover and simmer on low heat for 2 1/2 hours. Turn off the heat and allow the chicken to cool in the broth.

2   Skim solids from the broth and set aside.

3   Remove the chicken from the bone, cube the meat and set it aside. Melt the butter and add the flour, stirring until smooth. Cook for 3 minutes. Slowly pour in 5 cups of the chicken broth, stirring until it begins to thicken. If there is any broth left over, freeze it for later use. Add the chicken cubes, remaining celery, and the red pepper, parsley and salt. Simmer for 3-5 minutes.

4   Ladle into hot clean jars. Allow 1 inch of headspace. Cap and seal. Place in pressure canner on canning rack in 2-3 inches of water.

5   Lock lid in place and process for 75 minutes at high pressure. Let the pressure drop using the natural release method.

Servings: 4 pints

Headspace: 1 inch

Pressure Cooking Time
75 minutes / High Pressure

Pasta Sauce

Ingredients

5 pounds tomatoes cored and chopped
2 tablespoons olive oil
3/4 cup peeled, chopped onion
4 garlic cloves, peeled and minced
1/2 pound mushrooms, chopped
1/4 cup fresh parsley, chopped
1 1/2 teaspoons salt
2 bay leaves
2 teaspoons oregano
1 teaspoon black pepper
1/4 cup brown sugar

Directions

1 Place tomatoes in large saucepan and boil for 25 minutes uncovered. Allow cooling slightly then running through a food mill or sieving to remove skins and seeds.

2 In a large skillet, heat olive oil and sauté onions, garlic and mushrooms until tender. Place the sautéed vegetables in a stockpot, add tomatoes and remainder of ingredients and bring to a boil. Lower heat and simmer, uncovered for approx 25 minutes, stirring frequently to avoid burning.

3 Ladle into Jars. Allow 1 inch of headspace. Cap and seal. Place in pressure canner on canning rack in 2-3 inches of water.

4 Lock lid in place and process for 20 minutes at high pressure. Let the pressure drop using the natural release method.

Servings: 4 pints

Headspace: 1 inch

Pressure Cooking Time
20 minutes / High Pressure

Spicy Chili Sauce

Ingredients

6 long green chili peppers
2 large onions, peeled and chopped
8 garlic cloves, peeled and minced
4 tablespoons olive oil
7 tomatoes, peeled cored and chopped
1/2 cup tomato paste
1/4 cup lemon juice
1 tablespoon grated lemon peel
1 1/2 teaspoons salt
1 teaspoon dried coriander
Chili powder to taste

Directions

1 Place chili peppers on a baking sheet and broil for 30 minutes, turning occasionally to brown evenly. Remove from oven and allow to cool. Remove skins, stems and seeds. Puree them in a blender or food processor.

2 Sauté onions and garlic in the olive oil until tender. Combine onions, garlic and olive oil with chili pepper puree in saucepan with remaining ingredients. Bring to a boil. Reduce heat and simmer for 15 minutes or until thick.

3 Ladle into Jars. Cap and seal. Place in pressure canner on canning rack in 2-3 inches of water.

4 Lock lid in place and process for 35 minutes at high pressure. Let the pressure drop using the natural release method.

Servings: 4 pints

Headspace: 1/2 inch

Pressure Cooking Time
35 minutes / High Pressure

Barbeque Sauce

Ingredients

1 1/3 cup peeled, chopped onions
1 cup chopped celery
1 teaspoon of salt
1 1/4 teaspoon paprika
3 tablespoons mustard
3 tablespoons Worcestershire sauce
2 cups tomato paste
2 cups ketchup
22 ounces Water
2/3 cup distilled white vinegar
2 cups brown sugar

Servings: 4 pints

Headspace: 1 inch

Pressure Cooking Time
20 minutes / High Pressure

Directions

1 Combine all ingredients into a stockpot and bring to a boil. Lower heat and simmer for about 30 minutes, stirring constantly.

2 Once sauce has thickened, ladle into jars. Cap and seal. Place in pressure canner on canning rack in 2-3 inches of water.

3 Lock lid in place and process for 20 minutes at high pressure. Let the pressure drop using the natural release method.

Onion Salsa

Ingredients

4 onions, peeled and chopped
4 shallots, peeled and chopped
1 red bell pepper, seeded and chopped
2 tomatoes, peeled, cored, and chopped
1/2 cup lime juice
1/2 cup distilled white vinegar
1/3 cup olive oil
1/2 teaspoon cayenne pepper
1 tablespoon salt
1 teaspoon pepper

Servings: 4 pints

Headspace: 1/2 inch

Pressure Cooking Time
35 minutes / High Pressure

Directions

1 Combine all the ingredients and refrigerate for 48 hours. Place in a large saucepan, bring to a boil. Simmer for 5 minutes before ladling into jars. Leave 1/2 inch of headspace.

2 Cap and seal. Place in pressure canner on canning rack in 2-3 inches of water.

3 Lock lid in place and process for 35 minutes at high pressure. Let the pressure drop using the natural release method.

King or Dungeness Crab Meat

Ingredients

48 oz Crab Meat (12 oz per jar)
Lemon Juice
Salt

Servings: 4 pints

Headspace: 1 inch

Pressure Cooking Time
70 minutes / High Pressure

Directions

1   Keep live crabs on ice until ready to can. Wash crabs
    thoroughly, using several changes of cold water.
    Simmer crabs 20 minutes in water containing 1/4 cup
    of lemon juice and 2 tablespoons of salt per gallon.

2   Cool in cold water, drain, remove back shell, then
    remove meat from body and claws. Soak meat 2
    minutes in cold water containing 2 cups of lemon juice
    and 2 tablespoons of salt (or up to 1 cup of salt, if
    desired) per gallon.

3   Drain and squeeze meat to remove excess moisture.
    Fill jars with 12 ounces of crabmeat. Add 4
    tablespoons of lemon juice per pint jar. Add hot water,
    leaving 1 inch headspace.

4   Cap and seal. Place in pressure canner on canning
    rack in 2-3 inches of water.

5   Lock lid in place and process for 70 minutes at high
    pressure. Let the pressure drop using the natural
    release method.

Dill Pickles

Ingredients

1 dozen, 4" freshly picked
  cucumbers - sliced in quarters
1 1/2 cups vinegar, 5% acidity
2 1/4 cups water
1/4 cup non iodized salt
Dill (1 tablespoon per jar)
4 garlic cloves – 1 clove per jar
Mustard seed - 1 teaspoon per jar
Peppercorns -16 (4 per jar)

Servings: 4 pints

Headspace: 1/2 inch

Pressure Cooking Time
10 minutes / High Pressure

Directions

1   Place washed and sliced cucumbers in a large bowl.
    Cover with a layer of ice cubes and refrigerate for 4
    hours. Drain completely. Combine salt, vinegar and
    water. Heat to boiling.

2   Pack the cucumbers into 4 sterilized pint jars.
    Leave 1 inch headspace. Place dill, garlic, mustard
    seeds and peppercorns into each jar. Pour hot
    vinegar brine over cucumbers and spices in each
    jar, leaving 1/2 inch headspace.

3   Cap and seal. Place in pressure canner on canning
    rack in 2-3 inches of water.

4   Lock lid in place and process for 10 minutes at high
    pressure. Let the pressure drop using the natural
    release method.

Applesauce

Ingredients

7 pounds sweet, juicy apples
(for a tart flavor add 1-2 pounds of tart apples)
Ascorbic acid (to prevent browning)
Sugar & cinnamon mix to taste (optional)

Servings: 4 pints

Headspace: 1/2 inch

Pressure Cooking Time
8 minutes / High Pressure

Directions

1   Wash, peel, and core apples. Slice into water containing ascorbic acid to prevent browning.

2   Drain. Place drained slices in an 8-10 quart pot. Add 1 cup water. Stirring occasionally to prevent burning, heat quickly until tender (5 to 20 minutes, depending on maturity and variety). Press through a sieve or food mill, or skip the pressing step if you prefer chunk-style sauce. Sauce may be packed without sugar. However, if desired, add 1 tablespoon of sugar & cinnamon mix per pint of sauce. Taste and add more, if preferred. Reheat sauce to boiling.

3   Fill jars with hot sauce, leaving 1/2-inch headspace. Cap and seal. Place in pressure canner on canning rack in 2-3 inches of water.

4   Lock lid in place and process for 8 minutes at high pressure. Let the pressure drop using the natural release method.

Dried Apricot Jam

This jam can be made year round and is a delicious glaze for grilled meats.

Ingredients

1/2 pound dried apricots
2 cups crushed pineapple
  (well drained if using canned)
4 cups sugar
2 tablespoons
Fresh lemon juice

Servings: 4 half pint jars

Headspace: 1/2 inch

Pressure Cooking Time
5 + 5 minutes / High Pressure

Directions

1 Place the dried apricots in the pressure cooker and cover with water, about 2 cups. Lock the lid in place, bring to high pressure. Stabilize the pressure and cook for 5 minutes. Release the pressure. Transfer the cooked apricots to a large heavy pot.

2 In the heavy pot, mash the apricots with a potato masher and add the remaining ingredients. Stir well and cook over medium high heat until very thick, about 20 minutes. Ladle into jars leaving 1/2 inch of headspace.

3 Cap and seal. Place in pressure canner on canning rack in 2-3 inches of water. Lock lid in place and process for 5 minutes at high pressure. Let the pressure drop using the natural release method.

Citrus Cranberry Jam

This makes a tart and tangy holiday relish that can be made year round. It is wonderful with poultry and pork. Mixed with a bit of water or broth it makes a terrific cooking glaze.

Servings: 4 pint jars

Headspace: 1/2 inch

Pressure Cooking Time
10 minutes / High Pressure

Ingredients

2 - 12 oz bags of fresh cranberries
1 large grapefruit, about 1 pound
1 large orange, about 3/4 pound
1/3 cup dried pineapple, about 3 oz
1/2 cup dried cranberries
6 cups sugar
1/2 cup brandy

Directions

1 In a food processor, chop the fresh cranberries and dried pineapple. Transfer to a large stockpot.

2 Quarter the orange and grapefruit, remove the seeds, do not peel. Place in food processor and chop the entire fruit. Add to the pot with the cranberries. Stir in the dried cranberries, sugar and brandy. Stir until well combined. Bring to a boil, reduce heat and cook until thickened and no sugar crystals remain, about 45 minutes. Ladle into jars leaving 1/2 inch of headspace.

3 Cap and seal. Place in pressure canner on canning rack in 2-3 inches of water. Lock lid in place and process for 10 minutes at high pressure. Let the pressure drop using the natural release method.

Lemon Curd

This traditional style curd is a wonderful filling for small tarts and on hot scones. It must be eaten within 2 months.

Ingredients

3/4 cup butter
3/4 cup fresh lemon juice- about 6 lemons
Grated rind from the lemons
2 1/4 cups sugar
6 eggs, beaten

Directions

1
In a small, heavy saucepan over medium heat, melt the butter with the lemon juice and rind. Blend in the sugar. Stir until the sugar has dissolved. Whisk in the eggs and continue cooking until thickened. About 10 minutes. Stir constantly or the mixture can curdle.

2 Ladle into jars with 1/2 inch of head space. Cap and seal. Place in pressure canner on canning rack in 2-3 inches of water. Lock lid in place and process for 5 minutes at high pressure. Let the pressure drop using the natural release method.

Servings: 4 half pint jars

Headspace: 1/2 inch

Pressure Cooking Time
5 minutes / High Pressure

Creole Chicken

This is a wonderful excuse to celebrate Mardi Gras, even if you are not in New Orleans. The Filé powder acts as a mild thickener and gives an authentic Creole taste.

Ingredients

1/2 pound bacon, diced
4 cloves garlic, minced
1 bell pepper, diced
1 bunch green onions, diced
1 cup diced celery, about 3 ribs
1 teaspoon balsamic vinegar
1 tablespoon Worcestershire sauce
1 tablespoon Tabasco sauce
Pinch cinnamon
6 cans (14.5 ounces) diced tomatoes, do NOT drain

6 ounces chicken Anduille sausage, sliced
12 ounces chicken breast meat cut into 1 inch cubes

1 tablespoon Gumbo Filé powder*
1 teaspoon sugar

Directions

1 In the cooker set over medium heat, cook the bacon until crisp. Remove the bacon and set aside for later. Discard all but 4 tablespoons of the bacon drippings. In the reserved drippings, sauté the garlic, celery, bell pepper, and green onions until soft. Stir in the tomatoes, cinnamon, balsamic vinegar, Worcestershire sauce, and Tabasco sauce.

2 Lock the lid in place, bring to high pressure. Stabilize the pressure and cook for 15 minutes. Release the pressure. Stir in the meats and simmer about 15 minutes, or until cooked through. Stir in the sugar, reserved bacon and File' powder. Cook until slightly thickened.

3 Ladle into jars, leaving 1/2 inch head space. Cap and seal. Place in pressure canner on canning rack in 2-3 inches of water. Lock lid in place and process for 75 minutes at high pressure. Let the pressure drop using the natural release method.

Servings: 4 pint jars

Headspace: 1/2 inch

Pressure Cooking Time
15 + 75 minutes / High Pressure

Filé (pronounced "fee-lay") is a seasoning made from ground sassatras leaves.

Perfect Fresh Cream of Tomato Soup

This is the perfect way to use an abundance of fresh tomatoes from the garden.

Ingredients

2 1/2 cups of shallots, quartered
6 pounds of fresh tomatoes, quartered
1 1/2 teaspoons salt
1 1/2 teaspoons freshly ground pepper
1 1/2 teaspoons dried thyme
1/4 cup water
4 cloves garlic
1 cup cream, warmed (when serving)

Directions

1   In the pressure cooker, place the first 7 ingredients. Lock the lid in place, bring to high pressure. Stabilize the pressure and cook for 10 minutes. Release the pressure. The tomatoes should be completely soft and falling apart.

2   Run the tomato mixture through a food mill to remove the stems and seeds. Once the tomato mixture has been put through the food mill, place the soup in a sauce pan and keep warm.

3   Ladle into jars, leaving 1/2 inch head space. Cap and seal. Place in pressure canner on canning rack in 2-3 inches of water. Lock lid in place and process for 15 minutes at high pressure. Let the pressure drop using the natural release method.

4   To serve, reheat the soup and stir in 1/4 cup of warmed cream per pint jar.

Servings: 4 pint jars

Headspace: 1/2 inch

Pressure Cooking Time

10 + 15 minutes / High Pressure

desserts

Most people don't realize that truly delicious desserts can be made in a pressure cooker. From custards, flan, cheesecake, puddings, cake toppings and so much more! On the following pages, we've included just a few wonderful desserts for you to try in your Fagor Pressure Cooker.

Cinnamon Apple Flan
with Maple Syrup

Ingredients

5 tablespoons maple syrup

1 /4 teaspoon cinnamon

2 apples, peeled and cut in 1 /4 inch slices

3 whole eggs

3 egg yolks

1/4 teaspoon vanilla

6 tablespoons sugar

2 1/2 cups milk

Directions

1   In a small saucepan, combine the maple syrup and the cinnamon. Add the apple slices and slowly simmer until the apples are tender. Divide the mixture into 6 greased ramekins.

2   In a large bowl whisk the eggs and egg yolks. Stir in the vanilla, sugar and milk. Pour this mixture slowly into the ramekins.

3   Cover each ramekin tightly with foil.

4   Fill the cooker with 2 1/2 cups water. Place as many ramekins as will fit in the steamer basket and lower into the cooker onto the trivet. (Note: you can stack the ramekins in a pyramid to fit inside the cooker). Close the lid and bring to pressure.

5   Lock lid in place and cook for 6 minutes at high pressure. Let the pressure drop naturally, and keep closed for 10 minutes. Then remove the lid, take out the basket, loosen the foil on each ramekin and cool the custard.

6   Refrigerate. To serve, loosen the custard from the ramekins with a knife and invert on to dessert dishes.

Serves 6

Pressure Cooking Time
6 minutes

Pears stewed in white wine

Ingredients

2 cups water
1/2 cup sugar
2 slices lemon
2 cinnamon sticks
1/4 teaspoon ground mace
4 firm pears, peeled but not cored, stems on
3/4 cup red wine
1 cup frozen raspberries
4 tablespoons heavy cream

Directions

1   In the cooker, combine the water, sugar, lemon, cinnamon sticks and mace. Simmer until the sugar is dissolved.

2   Place the pears in the cooker, trimming the bottoms if necessary so they stand upright. Close the lid and bring to high pressure.

3   Cook for 2 minutes at high pressure. Release pressure and remove the lid. Add the red wine, close the lid and bring to pressure again. Complete cooking for 2 more minutes at high pressure. Release pressure and remove the lid.

4   Carefully lift out the pears and transfer to a deep container. Boil down the sauce until it is syrupy. Cool, then pour over the pears and keep at room temperature overnight.

5   To serve, defrost and puree the raspberries in a blender until smooth. Spoon 4 tablespoons of the puree on four dessert dishes or shallow bowls. Place a pear upright in the center of each dish. Spoon some syrup over the pears. Drizzle 1 tablespoon of cream in a circle over the sauce. With the aid of a knife, swirl the cream into the sauce to create an attractive design.

Serves 4

Pressure Cooking Time
2 minutes + 2 minutes

Pumpkin Custard

Ingredients

Butter-flavored cooking spray
1 cup canned pureed pumpkin
1/2 cup skim milk
1/3 cup dry milk powder
1 large egg white
1 tablespoon unbleached flour
2 tablespoons granulated sugar
3 tablespoons pure maple syrup
1 1/2 teaspoons pumpkin pie spice

Directions

1 Coat a pressure cooker baking dish with the cooking spray.

2 In a bowl, whisk together the pumpkin, milk, dry milk powder, egg, egg white, flour, sugar, maple syrup and pie spice. Pour into the prepared dish and cover it with a piece of heavy foil.

3 Place a trivet in the bottom of the pressure cooker. Pour in 2-inches of water. Lower the dish into the cooker.

4 Place lid on cooker and lock in place, bring to high pressure, stabilize and cook for 15 minutes.

5 Turn off stove and let the unit sit for 5 minutes, then release the pressure using the cold-water method. Carefully remove the lid.

6 Lift baking dish from the pressure cooker, remove foil covering and let custard cool to room temperature. Serve at room temperature.

Serves 4

Pressure Cooking Time
15 minutes

Pineapple Compote
with ice cream or pound cake

Ingredients

3 tablespoons butter

4 tablespoons brown sugar

3 cups crushed pineapple w/juice

3 tablespoons dark rum (or more to liking)

1/4 teaspoon vanilla extract

1 teaspoon cinnamon

1 quart vanilla ice cream or 1 loaf of pound cake

Directions

1 Melt butter, then add sugar. Stir.

2 Add the pineapple with juice (juice should be exactly 1/2 cup – if not, add enough water to amount of 1/2 cup), rum, extract and cinnamon.

3 Close lid, bring to high pressure, then stabilize pressure and cook for 3 minutes.

4 Release pressure, open lid, stir, and serve warm over vanilla ice cream or pound cake.

Serves 4-6

Pressure Cooking Time

3 minutes

Chocolate Mousse Cheesecake

Ingredients

1/2 cup chocolate wafer crumbs
1 pinch ground cinnamon
8 (1 ounce) squares semisweet chocolate
1 tablespoon butter
2 (8 ounce) packages cream cheese, softened
1 cup heavy whipping cream
1 teaspoon vanilla extract
2/3 cup white sugar
2 eggs, beaten
1 1/2 tablespoons unsweetened cocoa powder
1 1/2 cups water

Directions

1   Grease a pressure cooker baking dish. Mix chocolate wafer crumbs and cinnamon together. Sprinkle on the bottom of baking dish - pressing gently.

2   Melt chocolate and butter together and set aside.

3   Process cream cheese in food processor or electric mixer until very smooth. Add chocolate mixture and process until well-mixed. Add cream, vanilla extract, sugar and eggs, then cocoa powder until all ingredients are well incorporated.

4   Pour mixture over crumbs in baking dish. Cover entire dish with aluminum foil.

5   Add water to the bottom of the pressure cooker. Place the baking dish on a trivet in the pressure cooker. Close lid, bring up to high pressure, then lower heat and pressure cook for 50 minutes.

6   Remove cooker from heat, let pressure drop naturally. Remove cheesecake from cooker, and let cool to room temperature.

7   Remove cheesecake from pan, and refrigerate for 8 hours before serving.

Serves 12

Pressure Cooking Time
50 minutes

Creamy Cheesecake

Ingredients

1 tablespoon butter
2 teaspoons grated lemon zest
2 tablespoons flour
cookie crumbs
6 tablespoons sour cream
2 (8 ounce) packages of cream cheese
2 eggs
3/4 cup sugar
2 egg yolks
1/4 cup heavy cream
2 cups water
2 teaspoons vanilla extract

Serves 4

Pressure Cooking Time

30 minutes

Directions

1   Butter a pressure cooker baking dish. Sprinkle with cookie crumbs and set aside.

2   In a food processor, blend the cream cheese, sugar, cream, vanilla, lemon zest, flour, and sour cream. Beat in the eggs and egg yolks, pour into baking dish and cover with aluminum foil.

3   Pour 2 cups of water into the Pressure Cooker. Place the cheesecake in the Cooker Basket and lower into Cooker on top of a trivet. Close lid, bring to high pressure and cook for 30 minutes. Let the pressure drop naturally, remove the lid and take out the cheese cake. Loosen the foil, cool, then chill, preferably overnight. Spread fruit preserves in a thin layer over the cheesecake and serve.

Creamy Rice Pudding

*Once the rice pudding is cold, it can be sprinkled with sugar
and caramelized under the broiler.*

Ingredients

2 1/2 cups milk
1 cup rice
1 cinnamon stick
1/2 cup sugar
ground cinnamon

Directions

1   Put the milk, the stick of cinnamon, and the rice in the
pressure cooker. Cover, lock lid in place and bring to
high pressure. Stabilize pressure and cook for 6
minutes. Release the pressure.

2   Open the cooker, add the sugar, and heat and stir
until the sugar has dissolved.

3   Pour into individual bowls and dust with
ground cinnamon.

Serves 4

Pressure Cooking Time

6 minutes

Golden Apple Compote

Delicious over fresh baked gingerbread.

Ingredients

6 Golden apples, peeled, cored and cut into pieces
1 cup sugar
1 cup water
1 stick cinnamon

Optional:
zest of 1 orange and 1 lemon

Directions

1   Place the peeled and diced apples into the pressure cooker along with the water, sugar, cinnamon and zests, if desired.

2   Lock the lid in place, bring to high pressure. Stabilize the pressure and cook for 3 minutes. Release the pressure.

3   Place the fruit in a compote dish and serve at room temperature or cold.

Serves 6

Pressure Cooking Time
3 minutes

Holiday Compote

Serve this rich fruit melange by placing a pear half on a plate topped with the dried fruit mixture and softly whipped cream.

Ingredients

6 ounces mixed dried fruit
3 ounces raisins
6 ounces dried figs
12 dates
4 winter pears, peeled, cored and cut in half
1 cup sugar
1 cinnamon stick
zest of 1 orange
zest of 1 lemon

Directions

1   Place the dried fruit, raisins, figs, and dates in the pressure cooker with 1 cup water. Lock the lid in place, bring to high pressure. Stabilize the pressure and cook for 10 minutes. Release the pressure.

2   To the pressure cooker add the remaining ingredients and an additional 1/2 cup of water. Lock the lid in place, bring to high pressure. Stabilize the pressure and cook for 7 minutes. Release the pressure gradually. When cool, place in a bowl and serve.

Serves 8

Pressure Cooking Time
10 minutes + 7 minutes

Cherry Sorbet with Lime Sauce

It is a good idea to take the sorbet out of the freezer 30 minutes before serving. It will improve the flavor and will be easier to serve.

Ingredients

Sorbet:

1 pound of cherries, pitted (frozen can be used)
1 cup water
1/4 cup sugar
2 tablespoons fresh lemon juice

Lime sauce:

3/4 cup fresh lime juice (5 limes)
grated zest of 1 lime
1/2 cup sugar
3/4 cup water
2 tablespoons cornstarch (dissolved in 1/4 cup water)

Garnish:

4 almond wafers

Directions

1 Put the cherries in the pressure cooker with 1 cup water, sugar, and lemon juice. Lock the lid in place, bring to high pressure. Stabilize the pressure and cook for 3 minutes. Release the pressure. Purée the cherry mixture in a blender and chill in the refrigerator until very cold.

2 Pour the mixture into a rectangular mold and place in the freezer for 45 minutes. Take it out and beat it, breaking up any crystals that have formed. Put it back in the freezer for 30 minutes and then take it out and beat it again with the beater. (Alternately freeze in an ice cream maker according to the manufactures instructions). Store in the freezer.

3 To prepare the sauce, in a small cup dissolve the cornstarch in the 1/4 cup of water and set aside. Place the remaining ingredients in a heavy sauce pan and bring to a boil over high heat. Boil gently for 10 minutes. Stir in the dissolved cornstarch and cook until thickened and translucent. Pour the lime sauce into a small pitcher and let it cool.

4 Serve the sorbet in ice-cream ball shapes and garnish them with a little bit of the lime sauce. Serve accompanied with almond wafers.

Serves 4

Pressure Cooking Time
3 minutes

Caramelized Pears
with Red Fruits

This appears more complicated than it is. It is an elegant dessert that can be made ahead of time.

Ingredients

- 2 pomegranates
- 1 cup red wine
- 1 cup sugar, divided
- 2 cups water
- 4 winter pears
- 4 egg yolks
- 6 chocolate truffles or 6 ounces of chopped bittersweet chocolate
- 2 cups red fruits (strawberries, raspberries, diced plums)

Directions

1 Peel and seed the pomegranates. Marinate the seeds in the red wine while the pears are prepared.

2 In the pressure cooker combine 1/2 cup sugar with 2 cups of water. Peel, core and cut the pears in 1/2 vertically, and put them in the pressure cooker along with the sugar water mixture. Stir to coat. Cover, lock lid in place and bring to high pressure. Stabilize pressure and cook for 4 minutes. Release the pressure quickly. Remove the pears. Set the cooker aside for later.

3 Meanwhile, in the top of a double boiler, beat the egg yolks with the remaining 1/2 cup sugar until thick and lemon colored. Cook over boiling water until thick, stirring constantly. Remove from the heat and stir in the chocolate truffles until melted. Let cool slightly. Fill the pear cavities with the chocolate mixture. Arrange the pears on individual plates surrounded by the mixed red fruits.

4 Cook the syrup from the pears in the uncovered cooker until it has been reduced to a pale caramel. Be careful not to burn the mixture. Drizzle the hot caramel over the filled pears.

5 Pour the remaining caramel in the bowl with the pomegranates and wine, stir until well combined. Sprinkle the red fruits around each pear with a few pomegranate seeds and a little of the wine sauce.

Serves 8

Pressure Cooking Time

4 minutes

Bread and Walnut Flan

A slightly sweet bread pudding. This is a wonderful use for day old bread.

Ingredients

1/4 cup sugar
2 tablespoons water
4 slices bread, torn into pieces
1 cup milk
4 whole eggs
1 cup sugar
1/2 teaspoon cinnamon
1/4 teaspoon freshly ground cloves
2 tablespoons walnuts, chopped
2 tablespoons of raisins
2 tablespoons of brandy

Directions

1   Generously butter a pressure cooker baking dish. Prepare caramel by combining the 2 tablespoons of water and 1/4 cup of sugar in a small heavy saucepan. Bring to a boil and cook until the mixture just turns a light golden color. Remove from the heat. Be careful not to burn the mixture and handle with care. Coat the inside of the prepared baking dish with the caramel and set aside.

2   In a mixing bowl, place the bread, and cover with the milk to soften and set aside. More milk may be needed depending how dry the bread is. When the bread has softened, beat it with a beater until it is as soft and creamy as possible. Add the remaining ingredients and mix well. Pour the mixture into the baking dish and cover with buttered tin foil.

3   Place the dish on a trivet in the bottom of the pressure cooker with at least 1 inch of water in the base. Try not to have the water touching the base of the baking dish. Cover, lock lid in place and bring to high pressure.

4   Stabilize pressure and cook for 15 minutes. Let pressure drop naturally then refrigerate. Remove from the baking dish when it has cooled. Serve accompanied with whipped cream on the side.

Serves 8

Pressure Cooking Time
15 minutes

Peach Flower
with mascarpone cheese and nuts

This dessert can also be prepared with winter pears or Roma pears.

Ingredients

4 fresh peaches, ripe but firm
1/4 cup sugar
4 slices of pineapple in syrup (reserve syrup)
4 ounces mascarpone cheese
1 tablespoon sugar
3 tablespoons chopped nuts (walnuts, almonds, or hazelnuts)
juice of 1 lemon

Directions

1   Peel the peaches, make a knife slash around them and twist the two halves in opposite directions to remove the pit. Place the steamer basket in the pressure cooker, add the peaches to the steamer basket. Combine 2 cups of water, 1/4 cup sugar, and 1 tablespoon of lemon juice and pour over the peaches in the steamer basket. Cover, lock lid in place and bring to high pressure. Stabilize pressure and cook for 5 minutes. Release the pressure quickly.

2   Cut each peach half into thick wedges and cut the pineapple slices into 4 pieces. On each plate put 4 pieces of pineapple and the peach wedges, arranging them in a flower shape.

3   Beat the cheese with the tablespoon of sugar and make a rosette in the center with it. Decorate with the chopped nuts.

4   Cook 1/2 cup of the syrup from the pineapple with 1/2 cup of the juice from cooking the peaches. Reduce the liquid until it is a thick syrup, and just beginning to caramelize. Drizzle a bit of the syrup over the peaches.

Serves 4

Pressure Cooking Time
5 minutes

Heavenly Flan

This is very pretty garnished with whipped cream and diced candied fruits.

Ingredients

1/2 cup sugar
2 teaspoon water
4 eggs
1 cup milk
1 14 ounce can of sweetened condensed milk (use the can as a measuring cup)

Directions

1　Generously butter a pressure cooker baking dish. Prepare a caramel by combining the 2 tablespoons of water and 1/2 cup of sugar in a saucepan. Bring to a boil and cook until the mixture just turns a light golden color. Remove from the heat. Be careful not to burn the mixture and handle with care. Coat the inside of the prepared baking dish with the caramel and set aside.

2　In a mixing bowl, combine the sweetened condensed milk, milk and eggs and beat well. Pour into the prepared baking dish. Cover the baking dish with foil. Place the dish on a trivet in the bottom of the pressure cooker with at least 1 cup water in the base. Cover, lock lid in place and bring to high pressure. Stabilize pressure and cook for 15 minutes. Release the pressure, remove the baking dish and let cool at room temperature.

3　When completely cooled, remove from the dish by inverting onto a platter.

Serves 4-6

Pressure Cooking Time

15 minutes

225

Pineapple Praline Cheesecake with Caramel Sauce

Ingredients

1/4 cup butter, softened
1/3 cup light brown sugar, packed firmly
1/2 cup chopped pecans
1 11-ounce can pineapple tidbits, well drained
1 8-ounce package cream cheese, softened
1/2 cup sugar
1 teaspoon ground cinnamon
2 eggs
1/2 cup finely crushed gingersnap crumbs
2 cups water
Prepared caramel ice cream sundae sauce

Directions

1. Line pressure cooker baking dish with aluminum foil. Spread softened butter evenly over the bottom of the foil-lined dish, then sprinkle evenly with brown sugar and chopped pecans. Arrange pineapple tidbits over the top.

2. Beat cream cheese until smooth. Gradually beat in 1/2 cup sugar, cinnamon, then eggs, one at a time, beating well after each addition. Pour over pinaple tid bits. Sprinkle evenly with crumbs. Cover dish securely with aluminum foil.

3. Place 2 cups of water inside pressure cooker, place baking dish on a trivet, close lid and bring to high pressure, stabilize and cook for 20 minutes. Release pressure using the cold-water release method, open lid and remove baking dish. Allow to cool at room temperature then refrigerate until chilled.

4. To serve, drizzle caramel sauce decoratively over each serving plate. Place a slice of cheesecake over and serve.

Serves 6

Pressure Cooking Time
20 minutes

Warm Peach Dessert

Ingredients

3 tablespoons butter
4 tablespoons brown sugar
1/4 cup water
1 large bag of frozen peaches, defrosted
3 tablespoons dark rum (or more to liking)
3 teaspoons allspice
1 teaspoon ginger

Serves 4

Pressure Cooking Time

3 minutes

Directions

1   In the pressure cooker, melt butter, sugar and peaches. Stir.

2   Add the water, rum and spices.

3   Close lid, bring to high pressure, then stabilize pressure and cook for 3 minutes. Release pressure using automatic release method.

4   Open lid, stir, and serve over cubes of pound cake or ice cream.

Apple Raisin Bread Pudding

Ingredients

2 tablespoons butter
2 cups chopped cored cooking apples (about 2 medium)
3 cups day-old bread cubes (about 3 slices)
1/2 cup raisins
4 eggs
2 cups skim or low-fat milk
1/3 cup firmly packed brown sugar
1 teaspoon vanilla
3/4 teaspoon pumpkin pie spice
whipped cream or vanilla ice cream (optional)
apple wedges (optional)

Serves 8

Pressure Cooking Time
3 minutes

Directions

1   In pressure cooker, melt butter. Stir in chopped apples. Close lid, bring to high pressure, stabilize and cook for 3 minutes. Release pressure, open lid and add bread cubes and raisins.

2   In medium bowl, beat together eggs, milk, sugar, vanilla and spice until sugar is dissolved. Add in apple mixture and stir. Cover and refrigerate several hours or overnight.

3   In 1 1/2 quart casserole dish, bake mixture in preheated 350°F oven until knife inserted near center comes out clean (about 45-55 minutes).

4   Serve hot, warm or chilled, garnished with either whipped cream, ice cream and/or apple wedges, if desired.

Individual "Baked" Pears

Ingredients

2 large Bartlett pears, ripe but still firm
1/2 lemon
1/2 cup chopped walnuts
1/2 teaspoon cinnamon
1/4 cup brown sugar
1/2 cup dried currants or raisins

Garnish:
mint sprigs
vanilla Ice Cream (optional)

Directions

1   Place the steamer basket on a trivet the bottom of the cooker, add water to just below the basket. In a small bowl, combine the chopped walnuts, currants, cinnamon and sugar.

2   Halve the pears, peel and core. Rub all the surfaces with the cut side of the lemon. This will prevent the pears from browning. Cut 4 pieces of foil large enough to enclose each pear half. Place 1 pear, core side up, on each piece of foil. Fill the cavity with the nut mixture. Tightly seal each foil packet.

3   Place the foil packets in the steamer basket. Lock lid in place, bring to high pressure. Stabilize pressure and cook for 6 minutes. Release pressure. Remove the pears from the cooker. Unwrap each pear.

4   Immediately place each pear in a dish (can be garnished with a scoop of vanilla ice cream & the mint sprigs.)

Serves 4

Pressure Cooking Time
6 minutes

Lemon Cheesecake

Ingredients

1 teaspoon butter at room temperature,
  for greasing the baking dish
1/2 cup chocolate wafer or graham cracker crumbs
16 ounces cream cheese, at room temperature
1/2 cup granulated sugar
2 large eggs
1 tablespoon fresh lemon juice
1 to 2 teaspoons grated lemon zest
1/2 teaspoon vanilla extract

Directions

1 Grease bottom and sides of the pressure cooker baking dish with butter. Coat the sides with crumbs and distribute the remaining crumbs on the bottom.

2 Using an electric mixer or food processor, blend the cream cheese and sugar until smooth. Add the eggs, lemon juice and zest and vanilla. Pour the batter into the prepared baking dish.

3 Pour 2 cups water into a 6-quart or larger cooker. Set baking dish on a trivet in the bottom of the cooker to raise the cheesecake above water.

4 Lock the lid in place. Bring to high pressure. Stabilize pressure and cook for 15 minutes. Turn off the heat. Allow the pressure to drop naturally. Remove the lid, tilting it away from you to allow steam to escape.

5 Let the steam subside before lifting the baking dish from the cooker with the aid of the handle. If there is a small pool of condensed water in the middle of the cake, blot it up with a paper towel. Serve warm, or cool to room temperature, cover and refrigerate for at least 4 hours or overnight. Release and remove the rim of the baking dish. Can be served plain or with fresh fruit or cherry-pie filling on top.

Serves 8

Pressure Cooking Time
15 minutes

Quince-Apple Sauce

Ingredients

2 quince, peeled & cut in sixths
3 pounds apples, peeled & quartered
honey or sugar to taste
fresh lemon juice to taste
1/2 teaspoon ground cinnamon, cardamom, or allspice or
    a pinch of ground cloves, optional

Directions

1 Put the apples and quince into the pressure cooker,
add 1/3 cup water, cover and lock. Bring the pressure
to high, stabilize and cook for 10 minutes. Release the
pressure.

2 Puree the fruit with a hand mixer or potato masher.
Taste and sweeten with honey if the sauce is tart or
add the lemon juice if the apples are too sweet. Add
the spices.

3 Simmer for another 5 minutes to blend flavors,
then cool.

Serves 6

Pressure Cooking Time
10 minutes

Chocolate Crème Brûlée

A delicious indulgence for the chocoholic.

Ingredients

1 1/2 cups (12 ounces) of half and half
4 ounces dark chocolate, chopped coarsely
2 tablespoons sugar
1 teaspoon pure vanilla extract
1 cup egg substitute
2 teaspoons coffee liquor

Garnish:
4 tablespoons brown sugar, divided

Directions

1   Butter 4 ramekins and set aside. Place steamer basket on a trivet in the bottom of the pressure cooker and add water to just below the bottom of the trivet.

2   In a saucepan over medium heat, warm the half and half until bubbles just start to appear around the edges. Remove from the heat and stir in the chocolate until melted. Stir in the remaining ingredients. Pour the mixture into the prepared ramekins. Wrap each one tightly with aluminum foil and place them in the steamer basket on a trivet in the cooker. If the dishes won't fit in a single layer, they can be stacked pyramid style.

3   Lock the lid in place, bring to high pressure. Stabilize the pressure and cook for 23 minutes. Release the pressure. Carefully remove the foil wrapped dishes from the cooker, unwrap and cool to room temperature.

4   When cool, refrigerate until ready to serve. Sprinkle each custard with a tablespoon of brown sugar. Broil until the sugar has caramelized. Alternatively, a small kitchen torch can be used to caramelize the sugar. Serve immediately.

Serves 4

Pressure Cooking Time
23 minutes

Flourless White Chocolate Cake
with Rasberry Sauce

Impress you guests with this simple but elegant dessert.

Ingredients

Cake:

12 ounces white chocolate chips
3 tablespoons unsalted butter
3 eggs, at room temperature
1 tablespoon almond flavor liquor (such as Amaretto)

Sauce:

12 ounces fresh raspberries, divided
2 tablespoons honey
2 tablespoons water
2 tablespoons finely chopped almonds
mint sprigs for garnish

Directions

1 Prepare a pressure cooker baking dish by lining the bottom with wax paper and then buttering the paper and sides of the pan.

2 Melt the white chocolate with the butter in a saucepan and blend well. Whip the whole eggs for several minutes until tripled in volume. Stir in the Amaretto. Fold the eggs into the warm chocolate. Pour into the prepared pan. Wrap the dish in heavy duty foil. Place it on a trivet in the pressure cooker with 1 inch of water. Lock the lid in place, bring to high pressure. Stabilize the pressure and cook for 18 minutes. Release the pressure quickly.

3 Remove the pan from the cooker and unwrap. Cool to room temperature, then refrigerate. When cold, run a knife around the sides of the pan to loosen the cake, remove the sides and invert onto a serving platter. Peel off the waxed paper. The cake will be rather thin.

4 To make the sauce, place 6 ounces of the fresh berries in a small sauce pan with the honey and water. Bring to a simmer and cook until the berries are falling apart. Force through a small strainer to remove the seeds. Cool slightly and pour over the remaining whole berries. Stir in the minced almonds. Chill until ready to serve.

5 To serve, slice the cake with a thin knife. Pour a bit of raspberry sauce on a plate, add the cake and garnish with the mint.

Serves 6

Pressure Cooking Time
18 minutes

Index